WildFly: New Features

Get acquainted with the exciting new features that
WildFly has to offer

Filippe Costa Spolti

BIRMINGHAM - MUMBAI

WildFly: New Features

Copyright © 2014 Packt Publishing

First published: May 2014

Production Reference: 1190514

Published by Packt Publishing Ltd.
Livery Place
35 Livery Street
Birmingham B3 2PB, UK.

ISBN 978-1-78328-589-1

www.packtpub.com

Cover Image by Michal Jasej (milak6@wp.pl)

Credits

Author
Filippe Costa Spolti

Reviewers
Tomaž Cerar

Markus Eisele

Peter Johnson

Antonio Gomes Rodrigues

Commissioning Editor
Usha Iyer

Acquisition Editor
Mohammad Rizvi

Content Development Editor
Neil Alexander

Technical Editors
Novina Kewalramani

Pratish Soman

Copy Editors
Mradula Hegde

Laxmi Subramanian

Project Coordinator
Melita Lobo

Proofreaders
Simran Bhogal

Stephen Copestake

Indexers
Hemangini Bari

Tejal Soni

Production Coordinator
Komal Ramchandani

Cover Work
Komal Ramchandani

About the Author

Filippe Costa Spolti was born in Sao Joaquim, southern Brazil, considered one of the coldest cities in the country, but now lives in Minas Gerais. He works in the field of information technology and is a follower of the open source community. He contributes to open source projects, such as WildFly and Muffin. He currently works with management infrastructure in which the front-end is a park of physical and virtual servers running diverse critical business applications, and where he works mainly on the application servers, such as JBoss, Tomcat, and Apache. He is a professional, very flexible, and open to learning new technologies. He is a creator and maintainer of the hrStatus project, which is a free software for the DST Brazil. He is also currently working as an administrator of IBM PureSystems, which, by the way, was first deployed in Brazil and gave his company an international use case of the product.

I would like to dedicate this book to my father and thank everyone directly and indirectly involved throughout the production of the book, mainly the Packt Publishing team for giving me this opportunity.

About the Reviewers

Markus Eisele is a software architect, developer, and consultant. On a day-to-day basis, he works with customers as well as projects that deal with enterprise-level Java and infrastructures, including the Java platform and various web-related technologies, on a variety of platforms using products from different vendors. An expert in Java EE Servers, he is an Oracle ACE director, a Java champion, and a member of the Java EE 7 expert group, and is also a frequent speaker at industry conferences. You can follow him on Twitter (@myfear) or read his blog at http://blog.eisele.net.

> Sharing knowledge is rewarding. It also requires time, dedication, and motivation. I'm thankful that my parents taught me the foundations to be passionate and lasting; that my girls donate the time it takes and that I have a little power package to motivate me.

Peter Johnson has over 34 years' Enterprise-computing experience. He has been working with Java for 17 years. For the last 12 years, he has been heavily involved in Java performance tuning. He is a frequent speaker on Java performance topics at various conferences, including the Computer Measurement Group annual conference, JBoss World, and Linux World. He is a moderator for the IDE and WildFly/JBoss forums at Java Ranch. He is also the co-author of *JBoss in Action*, *Manning*, and has been a reviewer on numerous books on topics ranging from Java to Windows PowerShell.

Antonio Gomes Rodrigues earned his masters degree at the University of Paris VII in France. Since then he has worked with various companies having Java EE technologies in the roles of developer, technical leader, and technical manager of the offshore projects, and also as a performance expert.

He currently works in the APM area and is a performance problem fixer for an editor.

I would like to thank my wife, Aurélie, for her support, and my child, Timothée.

www.PacktPub.com

Support files, eBooks, discount offers, and more

You might want to visit www.PacktPub.com for support files and downloads related to your book.

Did you know that Packt offers eBook versions of every book published, with PDF and ePub files available? You can upgrade to the eBook version at www.PacktPub.com and as a print book customer, you are entitled to a discount on the eBook copy. Get in touch with us at service@packtpub.com for more details.

At www.PacktPub.com, you can also read a collection of free technical articles, sign up for a range of free newsletters and receive exclusive discounts and offers on Packt books and eBooks.

http://PacktLib.PacktPub.com

Do you need instant solutions to your IT questions? PacktLib is Packt's online digital book library. Here, you can access, read and search across Packt's entire library of books.

Why subscribe?

- Fully searchable across every book published by Packt
- Copy and paste, print and bookmark content
- On demand and accessible via web browser

Free access for Packt account holders

If you have an account with Packt at www.PacktPub.com, you can use this to access PacktLib today and view nine entirely free books. Simply use your login credentials for immediate access.

Table of Contents

Preface

The new WildFly application server, previously known as JBoss, has recently come up with several innovations and improvements in all its aspects. It is very lightweight, fast, and easy to implement and configure. In this book, we will dive into this new version of an established technology in order to know a little more about WildFly and find out what we will be able to do with it.

What this book covers

Chapter 1, Starting with WildFly, introduces you to this new technology giving the user a better understanding of the features present in WildFly, and this chapter will also show the reader how to perform a complete installation and will supply a brief introduction on how to do the main tasks. In addition, it gives you a complete idea of what the function of each directory is and the configuration file. At the end of this chapter, you should be able to perform a basic installation and configuration for implementing WildFly.

Chapter 2, Unified Configuration, explains that a good setting is the key to get the best of an application server in several aspects such as security, performance, and availability. Many configuration details sometimes go unnoticed but are fundamental. A great example is the default installation, which has been prepared to run quickly, and without many complications. Most of the time, it ends up being an Achilles heel and can cause problems in the future. By the end of this chapter, you will be able to implement the main settings in WildFly.

Chapter 3, *WildFly CLI and Management Console*, gives a brief introduction to the main settings that you can accomplish through management consoles. The management console and the CLI allow the user to connect the domain controller or a standalone server that gives us the option to perform all administrative tasks; only with the CLI, however, is it possible to execute all of them. The management console does not perform all the tasks. After this chapter, you will be able to use this tool and its main functions.

Chapter 4, *Modular Services and Class Loading*, is based on the JBoss modules. Instead of owning the hierarchy of the most known class loading, the WildFly class loading is based on modules that have to explicitly define the dependencies on other modules. By the end of this chapter, you will be able to understand how the class loader works.

Chapter 5, *Memory and Thread Pool Management*, explains that application tuning, JVM, and application servers in the Java world are very important points and can directly impact a production or development environment. We will see how the memory area is divided, what the function of each division is, and many other important concepts about this subject. By the end of this chapter, the reader will be able to measure their environment more efficiently.

Appendix, *What You Need to Know – Migrating from AS 7 to WildFly 8*, introduces you to the major changes that occurred between servers in JBoss AS 7 application, WildFly 8, and what you need to know to perform a migration.

What you need for this book

To make good use of this book and apply all the knowledge gained through, it is essential to have a machine with minimum requirements of 512 MB and 10 GB of hard disk space. A virtual machine with these settings is already good enough to begin learning. You also need to have a lot of interest to explore all that the book has to offer.

Who this book is for

The book will address the key subjects inherent in this technology that will provide the reader with important information to understand the application server and its main functions. The target audience for this book will be all the people who have interest in knowing the technology: administrators and developers. The book will address several issues; some subjects are superficial and others deeper to attract the reader's attention. The book does not let the contents become boring and uninteresting.

Conventions

In this book, you will find a number of styles of text that distinguish between different kinds of information. Here are some examples of these styles, and an explanation of their meaning.

Code words in text, database table names, folder names, filenames, file extensions, pathnames, dummy URLs, user input, and Twitter handles are shown as follows: "After installation, we must set the JAVA_HOME environment variable."

A block of code is set as follows:

```
<outbound-socket-binding name="gmailTest">
  <remote-destination host="smtp.gmail.com" port="993"/>
</outbound-socket-binding>
```

Any command-line input or output is written as follows:

```
[root@wfly_book opt]# cd /opt/
[root@wfly_book opt]# mkdir /opt/server
[root@wfly_book opt]# cd /opt/server
```

New terms and **important words** are shown in bold. Words that you see on the screen, in menus or dialog boxes for example, appear in the text like this: "Click on the **Profile** tab and then immediately click on **Datasources**."

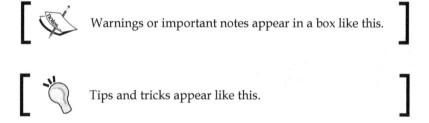

Warnings or important notes appear in a box like this.

Tips and tricks appear like this.

Reader feedback

Feedback from our readers is always welcome. Let us know what you think about this book—what you liked or may have disliked. Reader feedback is important for us to develop titles that you really get the most out of.

To send us general feedback, simply send an e-mail to feedback@packtpub.com, and mention the book title through the subject of your message.

If there is a topic that you have expertise in and you are interested in either writing or contributing to a book, see our author guide on www.packtpub.com/authors.

Customer support

Now that you are the proud owner of a Packt book, we have a number of things to help you to get the most from your purchase.

Downloading the example code

You can download the example code files for all Packt books you have purchased from your account at `http://www.packtpub.com`. If you purchased this book elsewhere, you can visit `http://www.packtpub.com/support` and register to have the files e-mailed directly to you.

Errata

Although we have taken every care to ensure the accuracy of our content, mistakes do happen. If you find a mistake in one of our books — maybe a mistake in the text or the code — we would be grateful if you would report this to us. By doing so, you can save other readers from frustration and help us improve subsequent versions of this book. If you find any errata, please report them by visiting `http://www.packtpub.com/submit-errata`, selecting your book, clicking on the **errata submission form** link, and entering the details of your errata. Once your errata are verified, your submission will be accepted and the errata will be uploaded on our website, or added to any list of existing errata, under the Errata section of that title. Any existing errata can be viewed by selecting your title from `http://www.packtpub.com/support`.

Piracy

Piracy of copyright material on the Internet is an ongoing problem across all media. At Packt, we take the protection of our copyright and licenses very seriously. If you come across any illegal copies of our works, in any form, on the Internet, please provide us with the location address or website name immediately so that we can pursue a remedy.

Please contact us at `copyright@packtpub.com` with a link to the suspected pirated material.

We appreciate your help in protecting our authors, and our ability to bring you valuable content.

Questions

You can contact us at `questions@packtpub.com` if you are having a problem with any aspect of the book, and we will do our best to address it.

1
Starting with WildFly

The book will address the key subjects inherent to this technology that will provide the reader with some important information, which will help them understand Wildfly Application Server and its main functions. The target audience for this book will be the people who have an interest in knowing the technology, mainly administrators and developers. The WildFly server is the same as Jboss AS7, but with numerous improvements and features, improved modularity, and better performance. It is really impressive when compared to previous versions such as Jboss 5 and even other Application Servers such as Weblogic, and has strong support from the community at `www.wildfly.org`. I hope the audience accepts and adopts the use of Wildfly since it is a new technology and is in fact a very promising application server.

What is WildFly?

WildFly, better known as JBoss Application Server, is a Java EE application developed entirely in Java, and thus can be run on any operating system, both 32 -bit and 64-bit. Some readers may wonder why JBoss had its name changed after so many years. This is due to a lot of confusion that was generated between the names of the products in their portfolio, and not only the JBoss application server, explains Jason Andersen, Director of Red Hat products. The name WildFly was selected by a vote initiated in October 2012, which was formally presented to the public in JUDCon Brazil 2013. The name WildFly was among other top-rated potential names such as basejump, Petasos, Jocron, and JBeret. But what really matters is its performance and ease of use. More details on the vote held by the company is available at `http://www.jboss.org/vote`.

The new WildFly has a highly optimized boot process; its services are started at the same time in order to eliminate the waiting time between the start of one service to the start of another, and all services that are not required at the time of startup are kept on standby until the time of first use. The main characteristics that it emphasizes on are connectivity, responsiveness, and scalability, and the main factor behind the improvements on these fronts is a new web server called Undertow,which is more powerful than its competitors such as Jetty Web Server. Its memory management is very aggressive in order to minimize the maximum allocation of heap memory. All the services used by WildFly use common indexed metadata cached to avoid the duplication of metadata. They also have modular load that prevents the loading of duplicate classes and has to be loaded over the system required for booting. All these factors not only reduce the overhead of heap memory but dramatically reduce the pauses made by the garbage collector (GC, this pause may be eliminated using the JVM settings) and also allow WildFly to run on devices with limited physical resources. WildFly implements the latest Java EE 7 specification that improve developer productivity by providing an easier way to develop modern Java EE applications, without requiring a combination of various existing frameworks, allowing a development team to operate with focus on the business of a company.

Hierarchical classloading often causes several problems, mainly library conflicts between different versions of the same library, but this ended in WildFly thanks to its modular structure that only links the **JAR** file to your application when it needs it.

Unlike most previous versions of JBoss, WildFly has all your settings centralized in a single file that is divided into subsystems that can be changed according to your needs; this becomes very useful if we are using a domain with multiple servers. In such cases, we have a centralized configuration in a single file. All the settings are based not only on edition of files; all management features are exposed through a Command Line Interface (that will be discussed in greater detail throughout this book), a web management interface, a native Java API, and through the Rest API-based HTTP / JSON and JMX. WildFly offers two execution modes: standalone and domain. The main difference between them is on the basis of scalability; the standalone mode works alone and the domain mode works with one or more servers.

WildFly practically supports all current Java EE 7 standards of web development and also features support for standards including JAX-RS, Java API, and it is also highly tolerant of server failures that give us support for clustering, session replication, and other services. WildFly also has a very large reduction in management and service ports, but is now going to have only two, application and management ports. The following screenshot gives a list of protocols that are supported along with the ports they utilize:

Port	Protocols	Bound Interface
9990	HTTP/JSON Management, HTTP Upgraded Remoting - (Native Management & JMX), Web Administration Console	management
8080	HTTP (Servlet, JAX-RS, JAX-WS), Web Sockets, HTTP Upgraded Remoting (EJB Invocation, Remote JNDI)	application
9999	Remoting - Native Management *(deprecated)*	management

Downloading WildFly

In addition to the final version, WildFly has several other alpha and beta versions mainly intended for testers whose primary purpose is to perform tests such as stress, load, response time, and so on. Furthermore, these versions allow the users to identify errors and bugs that are fixed in the next release.

Before starting the download, we must prepare the environment. For this book, the environment used will be as follows:

- CentOS-6.4-x86_64, available at http://wiki.centos.org/Download
- Choose the architecture now, choose any mirror, and then download the ISO file

With the operating system installed, we will download and install Java later. I advise you to always perform a manual installation and configuration of the latest available version. The Java SDK can be downloaded from http://www.oracle.com/technetwork/pt/java/javase/downloads/index.html.

In this case, I will be choosing to download the RPM version because we are using a RedHat-like operating system, as in an OS, which is based on the Red Hat Linux operating system, where the RPM is the native package manager. After the download, we will install and configure Java.

Installing Java

After you download Java and have already copied the file to our test server, we can now begin the Java installation.

1. Use the following command on the CentOS cmd:

```
[root@wfly-book ~]# rpm -ivh jdk-7u45-linux-x64.rpm
```

```
Preparing...                ########################################
# [100%]
    1:jdk                   ########################################
# [100%]
Unpacking JAR files...
        rt.jar...
        jsse.jar...
        charsets.jar...
        tools.jar...
        localedata.jar...
        jfxrt.jar...
```

2. After installation, we must set the JAVA_HOME environment variable:

3. Add the location of your Java installation under /etc/profile:

    ```
    Example:
    #Java configuration
    export JAVA_HOME="/usr/java/jdk1.7.0_45"
    export PATH="$PATH:$JAVA_HOME/bin"
    ```

4. Run the command below to apply the new configuration:

    ```
    [root@wfly_book ~]# source /etc/profile
    ```

5. To check the integrity of the installation, just run a simple Java command to verify:

    ```
    [root@wfly_book ~]# java -version
    java version "1.7.0_45"
    Java(TM) SE Runtime Environment (build 1.7.0_45-b18)
    Java HotSpot(TM) 64-Bit Server VM (build 24.45-b08, mixed mode)
    ```

With the Java installation completed successfully, we are now able to go to the next topic.

The installation guide and basic configuration

At this point, we assume that Java is correctly installed and configured as discussed in the previous section.

Now we are ready to download WildFly and start our installation. The download of the WildFly application server is available at http://wildfly.org/downloads/.

After the download completes and the file is sent to the server, we can initiate the installation. For this example, we will use a compressed version in the TGZ format, such as `wildfly-8.0.0.Final.tar.gz`.

First we must define a directory to perform the installation; one of the ways that I use to standardize my installation is by always using the following directory structure:

`/opt/server/{wfly_dir_name}`

Where {`wfly_dir_name`} is the name that you use to identify the instalation directory of your server.

Creating and accessing `/opt/server` using the following commands:

```
[root@wfly_book opt]# cd /opt/
[root@wfly_book opt]# mkdir /opt/server
[root@wfly_book opt]# cd /opt/server
```

Starting the WildFly extraction using the following commands:

```
[root@wfly_book server]# tar -xzvf /root/wildfly-8.0.0.Final.tar.gz
[root@wfly_book server]# ls
wildfly-8.0.0.Final
```

Note that the server directory has been created; we now have our WildFly application server installed. In the next topic, I'll talk a bit more about the installation and some basic settings, how to create a new user to access the management console and change the connection port numbers; we will also create a test application to perform a fresh deployment.

Before going on to the next step in which we will perform the first startup of the server, it is very interesting to understand how the subdirectories of WildFly are divided. The following are all the folders and their functions:

- `appclient`: Configuration files, deployment content, and writable areas used by the application client container are run from this installation.
- `bin`: All the server binaries, the startup script and also scripts that are used to setup the JVM startup parameters such as memory, heap memory size, among others, are present here.
- `docs`: In this directory, the license files, sample configurations, documentation, and other documents are located that will increase your knowledge about WildFfy.

- `domain`: This directory will only be used if the server is started in the domain mode. Inside are the settings files, deployments contents, and areas of writing used by the server to store log files and temporary files.

- `modules`: The WildFly classloading is structured in a modular way. All the necessary modules are stored in this directory. Also, the new modules that are installed should be stored here following the directory pattern. This directory should only be modified if you know what you're doing to avoid classloading issues.

- `standalone`: This directory will only be used when the server is started in the standalone mode. Here are configuration files, deployment contents, and areas of writing used by the server to store temporary files and logs, as well as the domain mode.

- `welcome-content`: This is an area of internal use of the server that should not be used by end users unless they want to overwrite and insert their own application in the / context. Its alteration can influence the functioning of WildFly, welcome pages, or error messages that are present in this directory.

With a prior understanding of the function of each directory present in the WildFly installation, it is also very important to have an understanding of each of the modes in which WildFly works as well as knowing your directory structure; the possible modes of execution are the domain and standalone modes. A short description about them is given in the upcoming section.

Content of WildFly standalone and domain modes

The following directories are part of the Wildfly filesystem:

- `Configuration`: It contains all the configuration files that are necessary to run this installation.

- `Deployments`: This is the directory utilized to perform your application deployments.

- `Lib/ext`: This is the location for installed library jars referenced by applications using the Extension-List mechanism.

- `Tmp`: These are the temporary files written by the server.

- `Data`: This directory is not present on the domain mode. Here are files written by the server during startup and their lifecycle.

- `Log`: These are the log files generated by the application server.
- `Content` (only for domain): This directory must not be modified by end users. Here the Host Controller is stored in the internal work area for this installation.
- `Servers` (only for domain): It is the writable area used by each application server instance that runs from this installation. Each application server instance will have its own subdirectory, created when the server is first started. In each server's subdirectory, there will be the following subdirectories:
  - `data`: This is the information written by the server that needs to survive a restart of the server
  - `log`: These are the server's log files
  - `tmp`: This is the location for temporary files written by the server
- `Tmp/auth` (only for domain): This is the special location used to exchange authentication tokens with local clients, so they can confirm that they are local to the running AS process.

Overview of the configuration files

Basically, the main difference is in the management of the two modes.

The domain mode does not accept exploded deployment. Also, the domain mode allows centralized management of all running instances to perform the deploys across all group instances simultaneously, which may cause application downtime during the deploy. Meanwhile, the standalone mode keeps each single instance as a single server instance and it is not necessary to have a more complex configuration for implementation; the deployment can be performed instance by instance. The following is a brief explanation of each configuration present in the each WildFly 8 installation:

The standalone mode

The relevant files used in the standalone mode are explained as follows:

- `application-roles.properties`: This is the file that contains the user permissions to access the applications. This file is changed by the user creation script that we will see later.

- `application-users.properties`: This is the file that contains user information and password to access applications. This file is changed by the user creation script that we will see later.

- `mgmt-users.properties`: This is the file that contains user information and password for access to the management console. This file is created by the user creation script available on the installation of the /bin directory.

- `mgmt-groups.properties`: This file contains group information and administration permissions that the users have. This file is created by the user creation script.

- `logging.properties`: This contains the initial bootstrap logging configuration for the AS instance. This boostrap logging configuration is replaced with the logging configuration specified in the standalone.xml file once the server boot has reached the point where that configuration is available.

- `standalone-full-ha.xml`: It is a Java Enterprise Edition 6 certified full-profile configuration file with a high availability and the full list of services.

- `standalone-ha.xml`: It is a Java Enterprise Edition 6 certified full-profile configuration file with high availability and the basic services.

- `standalone-full.xml`: It is a Java Enterprise Edition 6 full-profile certified configuration file that includes all the technologies required by the full-profile specification, including most other OSGI with the full services.

- `standalone.xml`: It is a Java Enterprise Edition 6 full-profile certified configuration file that includes all the technologies required by the Full Profile specification including most other OSGI with the full services.

The domain mode

The relevant files used in the domain mode are explained as follows:

- `application-users.properties`: This is the file that contains the user permissions to access the applications. This file is changed by the user creation script that we will see later.

- `application-roles.properties`: This is the file that contains user information and password to access applications. This file is changed by the user creation script that we will see later.

- `default-server-logging.properties`: These are additional logger configurations. The root logger will always be configured.

- `domain.xml`: It is a Java Enterprise Edition 6 full-profile certified configuration file that includes the technologies required by the full profile specification plus others including OSGi.

- `host-master.xml`: This contains all the information contained in the `host.xml` file; however, with a little difference, these configurations will be applied to the host master of the cluster. In the review of the file we have "*A simple configuration for a host controller that only acts as the master domain controller and does not itself directly control any servers.*"

- `host-slave.xml`: In this file, all the information that will be applied in the domain hosts slaves is present, that is., all instances of WildFly that make up the cluster.

- `host.xml`: This is the host controller configuration file for the installation. Each cluster member must have its `host.xml` file that contains particular information for each site. It must have information such as the name of the instance of the cluster, configurations about how a new member will contact the domain to register and access the domain configuration settings, as well as specific physical installation, for example, the name of the network interface that will be used for executing the WildFly.

- `logging.properties`: This contains the logging configuration for the host controller and process controller that run off this installation. It also defines the initial bootstrap logging configuration for each individual AS instance. This boostrap logging configuration is replaced with the logging configuration specified in the `domain.xml` file once the server boot has reached the point where that configuration is available.

- `mgmt-users.properties`: This is the file that contains user information and password for access to the management console. This file is created by the user creation script available on the installation of `/bin`.

- `mgmt-groups.properties`: This file contains group information and administration permissions that the users have; this file is created by the user creation script.

Now that you know a bit about the structure of WildFly directories and subdirectories, as well as their possible modes of execution and its main configuration files, you may also want to deepen the content of the `bin` directory. It is the directory that contains all the operations contained in the server. The main ones start and stop WildFly and many other files access the `bin` directory to check this out.

The contents of the directory may seem a bit lengthy, but it is actually because the scripts are duplicated except those inside init.d. In this case, it is only usable in Linux RedHat or Debian and the service folder that is designed only for Windows. Both are binaries needed to run the WildFly as a service; all others are duplicated. All scripts with the sh extension are for Linux and all with the bat extension are for Windows. Now we will study only the main scripts based on scripts only for Linux, since Windows will have the same function. The following is a brief explanation of the principal scripts and that will be mostly used in everyday life:

- add-user.sh: This is used to create an application or manage users that we will see later on in the chapter
- domain.sh: This is the domain mode startup script
- domain.conf: This is the boot configuration file that is used by domain.sh to set the boot parameters
- standalone.sh: This is the standalone mode startup script
- standalone.conf: This is the startup configuration file that is used by standalone.sh to set the boot parameters

The configuration files provide a little more detail. Instead of having the extension .conf, configuration files for Windows are terminated with .con f.bat.

Starting WildFly

WildFly has two execution modes, namely standalone and domain as previously described.

Starting the standalone mode

The following instructions will allow you to start WildFly in the standalone mode:

1. Go to the bin directory of the installation. If you do not remember, you can get their location through the environment variable set previously, as shown in the following command:

   ```
   [root@wfly_book ~]# echo $JBOSS_HOME
   /opt/server/wildfly-8.0.0.CR1
   ```

2. So just run the following command:

   ```
   [root@wfly_book ~]# cd $JBOSS_HOME/bin
   ```

3. And then run WildFly in the standalone mode through the standalone.sh script as follows:

   ```
   [root@wfly_book bin]# ./standalone.sh
   ```

Note that during the boot we received a little warning saying it was unable to obtain the hostname using the previous method (InetAddress.getLocalHost ()). This method searches the hostname configured on the local DNS server; on Linux systems it is located under /etc /hosts. See the following warning:

```
16:35:20,783 WARN   [com.arjuna.ats.arjuna] (Transaction Expired Entry
Monitor) ARJUNA012210: Unable to use InetAddress.getLocalHost() to
resolve address.
```

To solve this problem just add the hostname of the machine under /etc/hosts. There are two ways to do this. We can use the loopback address (127.0.0.1) or use the assigned address configured network interface (for example, eth0). For this example, we will use the network interface eth0.

To find your active interface type the following command:

- Linux: ifconfig
- Windows: ipconfig

These commands must be performed in a command-line tool (bash/cmd).

After the set up, the hosts file will look similar to the following lines of command:

```
127.0.0.1    localhost localhost.localdomain localhost4 localhost4.
localdomain4

::1          localhost localhost.localdomain localhost6 localhost6.
localdomain6

#ip              #Hostname

192.168.11.109   wfly_book
```

Now when you run the ping command, the hostname should respond by the configured IP address:

```
[root@wfly_book bin]# ping wfly_book
PING wfly_book (192.168.11.109) 56(84) bytes of data.
64 bytes from wfly_book (192.168.11.109): icmp_seq=1 ttl=64 time=0.023 ms
```

You can see that the warning we saw in the last startup did not occur again. If the startup at this moment occurred as expected without any error, it means that the settings made so far are correct.

Starting the domain mode

Assuming that the local directory is now /bin, run the following command:

```
[root@wfly_book bin]# ./domain.sh
```

Note that, unlike the standalone mode that starts only one process, in this mode we have four processes started by default. They are explained as follows:

- `Host Controller`: This process is the instance that acts as a central point of administration for all servers that are in the same domain
- `Process Controller`: This process is responsible for rehabilitating and monitoring other processes during its life cycle
- `Server One`: This is the process corresponding to the first server. It is the first instance of the WildFly domain
- `Server Two`: This is the process corresponding to the second server. It is the second instance of the WildFly domain

It is also important that we change the bind IP address of an application server, so we can access it from another machine. By default, WildFly will listen only on the loopback interface, or localhost, as shown in the following command:

```
tcp        0      0 127.0.0.1:8080              0.0.0.0:*
LISTEN        2745/Java
```

This information was acquired through the `netstat` command. You can also get this information through the server logs as shown in the following command:

```
18:42:29,119 INFO  [org.wildfly.extension.undertow] (MSC service thread
1-1) JBAS017519: Undertow HTTP listener default listening
on /127.0.0.1:8080
```

So we can change the `bind` address. We have two options to make this configuration. The first is by passing the parameter to the JVM and running the startup script from the command line or through the `standalone.conf` or `domain.conf` configuration files. The parameter responsible for this configuration is as follows:

```
jboss.bind.address
```

Downloading the example code

You can download the example code files for all Packt books you have purchased from your account at http://www.packtpub.com. If you purchased this book elsewhere, you can visit http://www.packtpub.com/support and register to have the files e-mailed directly to you.

To change the `bind` address only for one time, it can be changed for any purpose whatsoever. Pass the parameter in the startup script as follows:

```
[root@wfly_book bin]# ./standalone.sh -Djboss.bind.address=<your ip
address>
```

To permanently make this change so that every time the instance is started it remains active, we have two choices: using `standalone|domain.conf` or in the configuration file of the installation (`stanalone|domain.xml`).

In the `standalone|domain.conf` file, at the end of the next line add the configuration mentioned previously:

```
JAVA_OPTS="-Xms64m -Xmx512m -XX:MaxPermSize=256m -Djava.net.
preferIPv4Stack=true -Djboss.bind.address=<your ip address>"
```

And we also have the option to change the XML configuration file for the actual installation. This method is not very advisable, because the configuration file works with variables. The `jboss.bind.address` parameter is nothing but a variable that can be amended by passing a parameter to the JVM; if nothing is passed, WildFly will assume the default value for this and any other variable present in the configuration file.

To do this, change the variable value passing its IP address, as follows:

```
<interface name="public">
    <inet-address value="${jboss.bind.address:<your ip address>}"/>
</interface>
```

You can see that the `bind` address of WildFly now changes to what it was configured, using any of the ways mentioned earlier. Check the following part of the output:

```
19:13:05,888 INFO  [org.wildfly.extension.undertow] (MSC service
thread 1-1) JBAS017519: Undertow HTTP listener default listening
on /192.168.11.109:8080
```

And with the `netstat` command:

```
tcp        0        0 192.168.11.109:8080          0.0.0.0:*
LISTEN        3070/java
```

We will access the running instance through a browser of your choice with the IP that was set up. In my case, the IP is 192.168.11.109 and we have the following page displayed:

Other basic configurations

It is quite common in tests and production environments that we need to start more than one instance on the same server. WildFly has a very simple way to quickly set it. It is possible to start up an instance with all the doors changed very fast using a very convenient way. This configuration has a set of ports defined in the standalone xml / domain.xml configuration file; these define how many doors we want to add from the default ports. For example, if you want the next HTTP port to be 8081, just assign the value 1 instead of 0. If you want the port be 8090, simply assign the value 10, and so on. Here's how to make this setup simple. As an example, I will use the standalone.xml file.

Change the following line of code to turn the configuration permanent:

```
<socket-binding-group name="standard-sockets" default-
  interface="public" port-offset="${jboss.socket.binding.port-
    offset:0}">
```

Or just start the WildFly server passing these configurations as a parameter, as shown in the following command:

```
[root@wfly_book bin]# ./standalone.sh -Djboss.socket.binding.port-
offset=10
```

The part that should be changed is highlighted; instead of 0, we can insert any desired value that will be added to the default port. We will see the default ports shown in the following lines of command:

```
<socket-binding name="management-native" interface="management"
port="${jboss.management.native.port:9999}"/>

<socket-binding name="management-http" interface="management"
port="${jboss.management.http.port:9990}"/>

<socket-binding name="management-https" interface="management"
port="${jboss.management.https.port:9993}"/>

<socket-binding name="ajp" port="${jboss.ajp.port:8009}"/>

<socket-binding name="http" port="${jboss.http.port:8080}"/>

<socket-binding name="https" port="${jboss.https.port:8443}"/>

<socket-binding name="txn-recovery-environment" port="4712"/>

<socket-binding name="txn-status-manager" port="4713"/>
```

Once you perform the following change, including setting the value 10 instead of 0. It is as if we did all the changes manually, and it would look similar to the following code:

```
<socket-binding-group name="standard-sockets" default-interface="public"
port-offset="${jboss.socket.binding.port-offset:10}">

<socket-binding name="management-native" interface="management"
port="${jboss.management.native.port:10009}"/>

<socket-binding name="management-http" interface="management"
port="${jboss.management.http.port:10000}"/>
```

```
<socket-binding name="management-https" interface="management"
port="${jboss.management.https.port:10002}"/>

<socket-binding name="ajp" port="${jboss.ajp.port:8019}"/>

<socket-binding name="http" port="${jboss.http.port:8090}"/>

<socket-binding name="https" port="${jboss.https.port:8453}"/>

<socket-binding name="txn-recovery-environment" port="4802"/>

<socket-binding name="txn-status-manager" port="4803"/>
```

If we want to change only a port or more than a port through parameters during startup, it is very simple. We will change the default port to 9190 for the HTTP parameter passed when starting up the instance:

```
[root@wfly_book bin]# ./standalone.sh -Djboss.http.port=9190
```

The result is as shown in the following command:

```
JBAS017519: Undertow HTTP listener default listening on
/192.168.11.109:9190
```

This can also be done using the netstat command:

```
[root@wfly_book ~]# netstat -anp | grep java
tcp        0        0 192.168.11.109:9190              0.0.0.0:*
LISTEN        3713/Java
```

We now have the HTTP protocol listening on port 9190. You can change all the ports that WildFly uses, but each port has its own specific parameter and if you want to change them, you should assign the port for the parameter. The following is a list of all ports that can be changed using parameters:

- -Djboss.management.native.port=<desired_port>
- -Djboss.management.http.port=<desired_port>
- -Djboss.management.https.port=<desired_port>
- -Djboss.ajp.port=<desired_port>
- -Djboss.http.port=<desired_port>
- -Djboss.https.port=<desired_port>

Thus we can use the port we want in a very practical way.

In a new installation in Linux environments, it is quite common to use the root user. And often just leaving WildFly running with the root user is a security loophole, where WildFly has the root permissions on a server that is running and therefore can perform any operation that requires root permissions, such as shutting down the computer. An example of this was Versions 4 and 5 of JBoss where it is possible to perform a number of tasks that could compromise the functioning of the server, perform deployment of malicious applications, shutdown the server, obtain physical server information, and more. Since Version 7 of JBoss, it has became more complex, because now, management consoles in the new installation are protected in two ways., The first is with the address at which the interface is listening; by default, it is always the loopback address. The second protection is that, if a user needs to access a server that is not created, the web management console is inaccessible until the user is created and user passwords are protected by encryption. As a continuation of this chapter, we will learn how to run WildFly with a user, but without many privileges in our newly-configured environment.

The first step is to define a username and create it. In this case, to facilitate the identification of the user, I decided to create a user called `wildfly` because we can identify which applications this user owns.

The first step is to create the runtime user on the OS:

```
[root@wfly_book bin]# useradd wildfly -c "WildFly Server Runtime user"
```

The parameter `-c` is a comment that helps auditors and administrators to identify the user. If you do not want to change the password of the created user, it is not strictly necessary. However, if the password is not set for the user, he/she cannot log in unless you are already logged in as the rootuser. If you want to alter this, perform the following steps:

1. The first step is to change the password for the user using the following commands:

   ```
   [root@wfly_book bin]# passwd wildfly
   Changing password for user wildfly.
   New password: Exampl3@test
   Retype new password:
   passwd: all authentication tokens updated successfully.
   ```

2. The next step is to grant read/write permissions in the WildFly server directory installation.

It is necessary that the created user can run WildFly so that the user becomes the owner of the installation directory and its subdirectories. He/she will need to perform read/write operations in these directories. If we do not do this, the server will throw an exception during startup. as shown in the following command:

```
[wildfly@wfly_book bin]$ ./standalone.sh

=========================================================================


  JBoss Bootstrap Environment


  JBOSS_HOME: /opt/server/wildfly-8.0.0.CR1


  JAVA: /usr/java/jdk1.7.0_45/bin/java


  JAVA_OPTS:  -server -XX:+UseCompressedOops -Xms64m -Xmx512m
-XX:MaxPermSize=256m -Djava.net.preferIPv4Stack=true -Djboss.modules.
system.pkgs=org.jboss.byteman -Djava.awt.headless=true


=========================================================================


java.lang.IllegalArgumentException: Failed to instantiate class "org.
jboss.logmanager.handlers.PeriodicRotatingFileHandler" for handler "FILE"
...
Caused by: java.io.FileNotFoundException: /opt/server/wildfly-8.0.0.CR1/
standalone/log/server.log (Permission denied)
...
```

You can see that we have a permission error in the log file. This is because it is the first file that WildFly tries to write during startup. To solve this problem, we need to change the owner of the files as shown in the following command:

```
[root@wfly_book ~]# chown -R wildfly.wildfly /opt/server/wildfly-
8.0.0.CR1/
```

As you can see in the following commands, all the files currently belong to the root file:

```
[wildfly@wfly_book wildfly-8.0.0.CR1]$ ls -l
total 408
drwxr-xr-x. 3 root root   4096 Dec 22 04:12 appclient
drwxr-xr-x. 5 root root   4096 Jan  7 19:12 bin
-rw-r--r--. 1 root root   2451 Dec 22 04:12 copyright.txt
```

```
drwxr-xr-x. 4 root root    4096 Dec 22 04:12 docs
drwxr-xr-x. 7 root root    4096 Jan  7 17:24 domain
-rw-r--r--. 1 root root 351490 Dec 22 04:12 jboss-modules.jar
-rw-r--r--. 1 root root  26530 Dec 22 04:12 LICENSE.txt
drwxr-xr-x. 3 root root    4096 Dec 22 04:12 modules
-rw-r--r--. 1 root root   2356 Dec 22 04:12 README.txt
drwxr-xr-x. 8 root root    4096 Jan  7 16:35 standalone
drwxr-xr-x. 2 root root    4096 Jan  3 11:59 welcome-content
```

After running the previous command, note that the user `wildfly` is now the owner of all the files, as shown in the following commands:

```
[wildfly@wfly_book wildfly-8.0.0.CR1]$ ls -l
total 408
```

At this point, we can start the server with the user `wildfly` with no startup problems. Let's see what happens when we issue the following command:

```
JBAS015874: WildFly 8.0.0.CR1 "WildFly" started in 14358ms
```

The server starts successfully. Note that, when we see the process, the runtime user is `wildfly`, as shown in the following commands:

```
[root@wfly_book ~]# ps aux | grep java
wildfly   4033 13.4 56.0 1594376 136876 pts/0  S1+  01:07   0:08 /usr/
java/jdk1.7.0_45/bin/java -D[Standalone] -server -XX:+UseCompressedOops
-Xms64m -Xmx512m -XX:MaxPermSize=256m -Djava.net.preferIPv4Stack=true
-Djboss.modules.system.pkgs=org.jboss.byteman -Djava.awt.head

less=true -Dorg.jboss.boot.log.file=/opt/server/wildfly-8.0.0.CR1/
standalone/log/server.log -Dlogging.configuration=file:/opt/server/
wildfly-8.0.0.CR1/standalone/configuration/logging.properties -jar /
opt/server/wildfly-8.0.0.CR1/jboss-modules.jar -mp /opt/server/wildfly-
8.0.0.CR1/modules org.jboss.as.standalone -Djboss.home.dir=/opt/server/
wildfly-8.0.0.CR1 -Djboss.server.base.dir=/opt/server/wildfly-8.0.0.CR1/
standalone
```

Nowadays, we, mainly system administrators, have certain requirements to standardize our environments for easy understanding of how they are configured and consequently maintain a default on new installations.

One way to keep everything in order is to organize the applications by the services. The installation of WildFly comes with a pre-configured script for executing the server as a service. It is within the following directory:

```
$JBOSS_HOME/bin/init.d
```

To start, you must copy the configuration file wildfly.conf, present in the same directory, to /etc/default or simply make a symbolic link. In this case, I will make a symbolic link to the file wildlfy.conf as shown in the following commands:

```
[root@wfly_book init.d]# ln -s /opt/server/wildfly-8.0.0.CR1/bin/init.d/
wildfly.conf /etc/default/
[root@wfly_book init.d]# ls /etc/default/
nss   useradd  wildfly.conf
```

I am using CentOS, which is a RedHat-like operating system, and it will also make a symlink script wildfly-init.redhat.sh for /etc/init.d as shown in the following command:

```
[root@wfly_book init.d]# ln -s /opt/server/wildfly-8.0.0.CR1/bin/init.d/
wildfly-init-redhat.sh /etc/init.d/wildfly
```

Before starting the service WildFly, we must change the wildfly.conf file uncommenting the most important configurations; these configurations are shown in the following code:

```
JAVA_HOME=/usr/java/jdk1.7.0_45
JBOSS_USER=wildfly
JBOSS_MODE=standalone
JBOSS_CONFIG=standalone.xml
```

Let's try to start it now with the service command:

```
[root@wfly_book init.d]# service wildfly start
Starting wildfly:                                          [  OK  ]
```

And check the log using the following command:

```
JBAS015874: WildFly 8.0.0.CR1 "WildFly" started in 16362ms
```

And to stop the WildFly server, just run the following command:

```
[root@wfly_book init.d]# service wildfly stop
Stopping wildfly:                                          [  OK  ]
```

Summary

Since we already have our new application server configured, we will proceed to the next step; that is, to perform a deploy with a simple application and some more advanced settings about logs, datasources, installing new modules, and other useful features.

Knowing a lot about an application server is actually an important point and one that differentiates us from others when we impose some configuration that can improve performance and server security. This requires a deep knowledge of the directory structure and key files, settings, and functions. An administrator who does not know the application server will face many difficulties in solving a problem and finding the root cause. The resolution of problems in Java applications is complex. Why just know only one side of the coin? It is also necessary to know a bit of Java. Keeping a standard premises helps to maintain an organized environment; even if the environment has more than one administrator or a newly hired person, they will not have difficulty navigating the environment but will become familiar with it, because it follows a pattern.

2
Unified Configuration

Correct configuration is the key to getting the best out of an application server in several aspects such as security, performance, and availability. Many configuration details sometimes go unnoticed and are fundamental. A great example is the default installation, which has been prepared to run quickly and without many complications. This can often end up being an Achilles heel and can cause problems in the future.

Running our first web application

Before we begin, I will describe the activities that need to be performed, and configuration that needs to be done, on the server to execute the deployment of a simple application that will be used in this chapter to illustrate a basic deployment. This application will be used to accomplish a few more settings, such as context root and virtual host. Also, I will describe a little about deployment into a single standalone server and, in some server instances, running in the domain mode. For the domain mode deployments, you should proceed to *Chapter 3*, *WildFly CLI and Management Console*.

The `standalone/deployments` directory, as in the previous releases of JBoss Application Server, is the location used by end users to perform their deployments and applications are automatically deployed into the server at runtime. The artifacts that can be used to deploy are as follows:

- WAR (Web application Archive): This is a JAR file used to distribute a collection of JSP (Java Server Pages), servlets, Java classes, XML files, libraries, static web pages, and several other features that make up a web application.

- EAR (Enterprise Archive): This type of file is used by Java EE for packaging one or more modules within a single file.

- JAR (Java Archive): This is used to package multiple Java classes.

- RAR (Resource Adapter Archive): This ia an archive file that is defined in the JCA specification as the valid format for deployment of resource adapters on application servers. You can deploy a RAR file on the AS Java as a standalone component or as part of a larger application. In both cases, the adapter is available to all applications using a lookup procedure.

The deployment in WildFly has some deployment file markers that can be identified quickly, both by us and by WildFly, to understand what is the status of the artifact, whether it was deployed or not. The file markers always have the same name as the artifact that will deploy. A basic example is the marker used to indicate that `my-first-app.war`, a deployed application, will be the `dodeploy` suffix. Then in the directory to deploy, there will be a file created with the name `my-first-app.war.dodeploy`. Among these markers, there are others, explained as follows:

- `dodeploy`: This suffix is inserted by the user, which indicates that the deployment scanner will deploy the artifact indicated. This marker is mostly important for exploded deployments.

- `skipdeploy`: This marker disables the autodeploy mode while this file is present in the deploy directory, only for the artifact indicated.

- `isdeploying`: This marker is placed by the deployment scanner service to indicate that it has noticed a `.dodeploy` file or a new or updated autodeploy mode and is in the process of deploying the content. This file will be erased by the deployment scanner so the deployment process finishes.

- `deployed`: This marker is created by the deployment scanner to indicate that the content was deployed in the runtime.

- `failed`: This marker is created by the deployment scanner to indicate that the deployment process failed.

- `isundeploying`: This marker is created by the deployment scanner and indicates the file suffix `.deployed` was deleted and its contents will be undeployed. This marker will be deleted when the process is completely undeployed.

- `undeployed`: This marker is created by the deployment scanner to indicate that the content was undeployed from the runtime.

- `pending`: This marker is placed by the deployment scanner service to indicate that it has noticed the need to deploy content but has not yet instructed the server to deploy it.

When we deploy our first application, we'll see some of these marker files, making it easier to understand their functions. To support learning, the small applications that I made will be available on GitHub (https://github.com) and packaged using Maven (for further details about Maven, you can visit http://maven.apache.org/). To begin the deployment process, we perform a checkout of the first application.

1. First of all you need to install the Git client for Linux. To do this, use the following command:

   ```
   [root@wfly_book ~]# yum install git -y
   ```

2. Git is also necessary to perform the Maven installation so that it is possible to perform the packaging process of our first application. Maven can be downloaded from http://maven.apache.org/download.cgi.

3. Once the download is complete, create a directory that will be used to perform the installation of Maven and unzip it into this directory. In my case, I chose the folder /opt as follows:

   ```
   [root@wfly_book ~]# mkdir /opt/maven
   ```

4. Unzip the file into the newly created directory as follows:

   ```
   [root@wfly_book maven]# tar -xzvf /root/apache-maven-3.2.1-bin.tar.gz

   [root@wfly_book maven]# cd apache-maven-3.2.1/
   ```

5. Run the mvn command and, if any errors are returned, we must set the environment variable M3_HOME, described as follows:

   ```
   [root@wfly_book ~]# mvn

   -bash: mvn: command not found
   ```

6. If the error indicated previously occurs again, it is because the Maven binary was not found by the operating system; in this scenario, we must create and configure the environment variable that is responsible for this. First, two settings, populate the environment variable with the Maven installation directory and enter the directory in the PATH environment variable in the necessary binaries.

7. Access and edit the /etc/profile file, taking advantage of the configuration that we did earlier with the Java environment variable, and see how it will look with the Maven configuration file as well:

   ```
   #Java and Maven configuration
   export JAVA_HOME="/usr/java/jdk1.7.0_45"
   export M3_HOME="/opt/maven/apache-maven-3.2.1"
   export PATH="$PATH:$JAVA_HOME/bin:$M3_HOME/bin"
   ```

8. Save and close the file and then run the following command to apply the following settings:

```
[root@wfly_book ~]# source /etc/profile
```

9. To verify the configuration performed, run the following command:

```
[root@wfly_book ~]# mvn -version
```

10. Well, now that we have the necessary tools to check out the application, let's begin. First, set a directory where the application's source codes will be saved as shown in the following command:

```
[root@wfly_book opt]# mkdir book_apps
[root@wfly_book opt]# cd book_apps/
```

11. Let's check out the project using the command, git clone; the repository is available at https://github.com/spolti/wfly_book.git. Perform the checkout using the following command:

```
[root@wfly_book book_apps]# git clone https://github.com/spolti/
wfly_book.git
```

12. Access the newly created directory using the following command:

```
[root@wfly_book book_apps]# cd wfly_book/
```

For the first example, we will use the application called app1-v01, so access this directory and build and deploy the project by issuing the following commands. Make sure that the WildFly server is already running.

The first build is always very time-consuming, because Maven will download all the necessary libs to compile the project, project dependencies, and Maven libraries.

```
[root@wfly_book wfly_book]# cd app1-v01/
[root@wfly_book app1-v01]# mvn wildfly:deploy
```

For more details about the WildFly Maven plugin, please take a look at https://docs.jboss.org/wildfly/plugins/maven/latest/index.html.

The artifact will be generated and automatically deployed on WildFly Server.

Note that a message similar to the following is displayed stating that the application was successfully deployed:

```
INFO  [org.jboss.as.server] (ServerService Thread Pool -- 29) JBAS018559:
Deployed "app1-v01.war" (runtime-name : "app1-v01.war")
```

When we perform the deployment of some artifact, and if we have not configured the virtual host or context root address, then in order to access the application we always need to use the application name without the suffix, because our application's address will be used for accessing it. The structure to access the application is `http://<your -ip-address>:<port-number>/app1-v01/`.

In my case, it would be `http://192.168.11.109:8080/app1-v01/`.

See the following screenshot of the application running. This application is very simple and is made using JSP and rescuing some system properties.

Note that in the deployments directory we have a marker file that indicates that the application was successfully deployed, as follows:

```
[root@wfly_book deployments]# ls -l
total 20
-rw-r--r--. 1 wildfly wildfly 2544 Jan 21 07:33 app1-v01.war
-rw-r--r--. 1 wildfly wildfly   12 Jan 21 07:33 app1-v01.war.deployed
-rw-r--r--. 1 wildfly wildfly 8870 Dec 22 04:12 README.txt
```

To undeploy the application without having to remove the artifact, we need only remove the `app1-v01.war.deployed` file. This is done using the following command:

```
[root@wfly_book ~]# cd $JBOSS_HOME/standalone/deployments
[root@wfly_book deployments]# rm app1-v01.war.deployed
rm: remove regular file `app1-v01.war.deployed'? y
```

In the previous option, you will also need to press Y to remove the file. You can also use the WildFly Maven plugin for undeployment, using the following command:

```
[root@wfly_book deployments]# mvn wildfly:undeploy
```

Notice that the log is reporting that the application was undeployed and also note that a new marker, .undeployed, has been added indicating that the artifact is no longer active in the runtime server as follows:

```
INFO  [org.jboss.as.server] (DeploymentScanner-threads - 1) JBAS018558:
Undeployed "app1-v01.war" (runtime-name: "app1-v01.war")
```

And run the following command:

```
[root@wfly_book deployments]# ls -l
total 20
-rw-r--r--. 1 wildfly wildfly 2544 Jan 21 07:33 app1-v01.war
-rw-r--r--. 1 wildfly wildfly   12 Jan 21 09:44 app1-v01.war.undeployed
-rw-r--r--. 1 wildfly wildfly 8870 Dec 22 04:12 README.txt
[root@wfly_book deployments]#
```

If you make undeploy using the WildFly Maven plugin, the artifact will be deleted from the deployments directory.

Throughout this chapter, we will learn how to configure an application using a virtual host, the context root, and also how to use the logging tools that we now have available to use Java in some of our test applications, among several other very interesting settings.

Changing the application context root

The context root or URI is a simple way to keep a friendly name for our applications when calls are made via the browser. When WildFly does a deployment, it checks if this setting is enabled in the application and then interprets the configuration, registering the application with the context root configured. It is very useful when you have a versioned application. In order to keep the version in the filename for easier understanding and standardization, the application gets a very long name. For example, if an application had the name intranet-0.0.1-Final and did not have the context root configured, the application should be called using the entire file name; however, we want the application be called only with a much simpler context root (for example, /intranet/).

Now we will see how to configure the context root of the application.

To perform this configuration it is necessary to create a new file within the application's WEB-INF folder; this is the same directory where the web.xml file is located.

This setting is made for a file called `jboss-web.xml` that should be placed in the `WEB-INF` directory with the following code:

```
<?xml version="1.0" encoding="UTF-8" ?>
<jboss-web>
  <context-root>/app1-v02</context-root>
</jboss-web>
```

If you are running an EAR application, you can do this through the `application.xml` file under the `META-INF` directory, as follows:

```
<application xmlns="http://java.sun.com/xml/ns/j2ee" version="1.4"
    xmlns:xsi="http://www.w3.org/2001/XMLSchema-instance"
    xsi:schemaLocation="http://java.sun.com /xml/ns/j2ee
                        http://java.sun.com/xml/ns/j2ee/
application_1_4.xsd">

  <module>
    <web>
      <web-uri>app1-v01.war</web-uri>
      <context-root>/app1-v02</context-root>
    </web>
  </module>

</application>
```

To perform the deploy and see this configuration running, we will do the build of the application, `app1-v02`. In order to do that, access the directory and deploy the project with Maven, as follows:

1. First access the directory of the second application:

    `[root@wfly_book ~]# cd /opt/book_apps/wfly_book/app1-v02/`

2. Then build the project with Maven:

    `[root@wfly_book app1-v02]# mvn wildfly:deploy`

Note in the logs that, despite the artifact name (`app1-v02-0.0.1-SNAPSHOT.war`), the context recorded by WildFly was `/app1-v02`, so just use this to access the application. The output is as follows:

```
INFO  [org.jboss.as.server.deployment] (MSC service thread 1-2)
JBAS015876: Starting deployment of "app1-v02-0.0.1-SNAPSHOT.war"
(runtime-name: "app1-v02-0.0.1-SNAPSHOT.war")

2014-01-21 10:14:05,771 INFO  [org.wildfly.extension.undertow] (MSC
service thread 1-1) JBAS017534: Register web context: /app1-v02
```

As you can see in the following screenshot, an access is performed using the context root configured:

You can also configure the application so that it is accessed without specifying the URI. For this example, we will use the same prior application; let's just change the file that defines this configuration and run the application deploy again. Change the file jboss-web.xml using the following command:

```
[root@wfly_book deployments]# gedit /opt/book_apps/wfly_book/app1-v02/
src/main/webapp/WEB-INF/jboss-web.xml
```

Modify this file as follows:

```
<?xml version="1.0" encoding="UTF-8" ?>
<jboss-web>
    <context-root>/</context-root>
</jboss-web>
```

The following steps will show how to configure the context root of your application to be accessed by the / context:

1. So, let's build the artifact again and perform deploy. This time we will use the markers files to undeploy the previous application and perform deploy on the modified application. Access the application's root directory and then run the Maven deploy with one more parameter, clean, to clean old build data from the previous build, as follows:

    ```
    [root@wfly_book deployments]# cd /opt/book_apps/wfly_book/
    app1-v02/
    ```

2. Before you build the app, run the undeploy command:

```
[root@wfly_book app1-v02]# mvn wildfly:undeploy
```

3. Then, execute the new deployment:

```
[root@wfly_book app1-v02]# mvn clean wildfly:deploy
```

Now, access the application using only the IP address and the port of the server, as shown in the following screenshot:

Configuring a virtual host

In application servers, virtual hosts have their importance; virtually, all sites that have accessed Java virtual hosts configured. In WildFly, an instance can have multiple virtual hosts and can also use aliases for a virtual host. It can thus be accessed by more than one name. The configuration that defines it consists of three steps; the first step is to configure the application in the jboss-web.xml file with the virtual host entry. The next step is to configure the virtual host on the application server; it must be exactly the same as configured in the application. Finally, you need to add a record in **DNS (Domain Name System)** so that, when you access the virtual host, it is translated to IP.

The first step is simple; you must configure the jboss-web.xml file. It is used to change the context root of the application, as we have seen in the previous example, by inserting just one more record to complete the first part of the setup; you can see how simple it is in the following code:

```
<?xml version="1.0" encoding="UTF-8" ?>
<jboss-web>
```

```
        <context-root>/</context-root>
        <virtual-host>app1-host</virtual-host>
</jboss-web>
```

The virtual host field should be populated with the name of the application you want to access. In this case, as configured previously, we can access the application using only the name app1-v03 or typing this name to a domain, but the domain to use it must also be configured as an alias on the virtual host of the application server configuration.

The configuration we made previously is necessary to prepare WildFly to treat the virtual host. In this case, we will use the standalone mode; so let's edit the configuration file, standalone.xml, as follows:

```
[root@wfly_book deployments]# vim /opt/server/wildfly-8.0.0.CR1/
standalone/configuration/standalone.xml
```

Locate the following line of code:

```
<subsystem xmlns="urn:jboss:domain:undertow:1.0">
```

Between the <server> tags and </ server> tags, add the following entry:

```
<host name="app1-host" alias="app1-host.mydomain.com" default
-web-module="app1-v03" />
```

In the previous entry, you need to make sure of the following points:

- **name**: This is the same name configured in jboss-web.xml of the application on the host's virtual tag.

- **alias**: This is an alias that may also be called to access the application. One virtual host can have more than one alias separated by a comma (,).

- **default-web-module**: This is the artifact name without the suffix. It is usually WAR in applications that are built with Maven, which is the case in our example. You should use the value that is in the artifact-id field in the pom.xml file of the project.

After the previous steps are performed, the configuration of the virtual host and the Undertow subsystem will look exactly like the following code:

```
<server name="default-server">
      <http-listener name="default" socket-binding="http"/>
      <host name="default-host" alias="localhost">
         <location name="/" handler="welcome-content"/>
      </host>
```

```
    <host name="app1-v03" alias="app1-v03.mydomain.com" default-
    web-module="app1-v03" />
</server>
```

The configuration of our virtual host is highlighted in the previous code snippet.

And lastly, we should configure the virtual host created in our DNS. As it is a test environment and probably does not have a DNS configured, just change the local DNS of the machine present, in this case, within the host's file located in the following directories:

- **Linux**: `/etc/hosts`
- **Windows**: `C:\WINDOWS\system32\drivers\etc\hosts`

Insert a new record in the file by following the ensuing pattern:

```
<your-server-ip-adrres>   <your-virtual-host-alias|name>
```

In my case, this is done as follows:

```
192.168.11.109  app1-v03.mydomain.com
```

To make sure that the DNS configuration is correct, simply ping the domain and see if it will respond with the correct IP address. Use the `ping` command from a command line window as follows:

```
C:\Documents and Settings\Filippe>ping app1-v03.mydomain.com


PING app1-v03.mydomain.com [192.168.11.109] com 32 bytes of data:


Reply from 192.168.11.109: bytes=32 time<1ms TTL=64
Reply from 192.168.11.109: bytes=32 time<1ms TTL=64
Reply from 192.168.11.109: bytes=32 time<1ms TTL=64
Reply from 192.168.11.109: bytes=32 time<1ms TTL=64


Ping statistics to 192.168.11.109:
    Packets: transmitted = 4, received = 4, loss = 0 (0% loss),
```

Now that the settings have already been made, we can build and deploy the third sample application that is in the same directory as the previous one; access it using the following commands:

```
[root@wfly_book deployments]# cd /opt/book_apps/wfly_book/app1-v03/
```

```
[root@wfly_book app1-v03]# mvn wildfly:deploy


INFO  [org.wildfly.extension.undertow]  (MSC service thread 1-2)
JBAS017531: Host app1-v03 starting
```

Note that the log mentions that the virtual host was started successfully. Well, we can now access our application using the previously configured virtual host, as shown in the following screenshot:

Our next step will be to learn to use the logging tool in WildFly, `log4j`.

WildFly logging

The logging service is extremely important for any type of application server and also other types of servers. It is through it that we can check on the status of the application server and also the applications. The resolution of errors is also directly linked to the logs because it is through them that we know which errors are occurring and from there can look for a solution.

The configuration of logging in WildFly is done by the logging subsystem that is configured in the `standalone.xml` files when we're running standalone and in `domain.xml` files when we're running in the domain mode.

The logging subsystem has three main components that we should be aware of:

- **Handlers**: These define how a particular event is logged. We have the following handlers:
  - ○ **Console**: This handler records events only in the currently open console. If no console is available, it will not print generated log events for this handler.
  - ○ **File**: This handler registers the events in a file. It is possible to create other custom handlers. For example, if we need to save the events of a particular application or context, we can create a handler for this. We'll see how this configuration is done during this topic.

- **Loggers**: It is useful to arrange the logs by categories; for example, you can enable the logging level to debug only one class or backdrop. This will be looked into throughout this topic.

- **Root Logger**: The root logger is at the top of the logger hierarchy tree.

The logging service also has logging levels, which are very interesting because they are defined by the criticality level of the log being printed, or if it is only information or more detailed logs in order to effect a debug of what is happening on the server. We have the following logging levels:

- **FATAL**: It indicates that some very critical problems occurred on the server and the service cannot continue to run.

- **ERROR**: This shows that an error occurred at runtime, but this error does not prevent the server or the application from continuing to run.

- **WARN**: This type of event warns that something wrong was found; however, it is not so critical that it can cause some damage at runtime.

- **INFO**: This level prints only information from the server or application

- **DEBUG**: Extra information used for debugging; it is used to perform troubleshooting and is also used by developers.

- **TRACE**: This level allows a detailed analysis of the server. This is the most detailed level of logging. It is not recommended to use it in a production environment because if this level is enabled, WildFly will write numerous lines in the log file generating a lot of I/O, which can compromise the performance of the server. This issue applies to the debug level as well.

The logs have hierarchical levels, the most critical to less critical. This hierarchy has the following order:

FATAL -> ERROR -> WARN -> INFO -> DEBUG -> TRACE

That is, if we enable the **TRACE** level all levels are printed.

If we enable the DEBUG level, it will print only the DEBUG, INFO, WARN, ERROR, and FATAL levels.

By default, this setting is initially configured with the INFO level, so it will print only INFO, WARN, ERROR, and FATAL levels. For production environments, it is recommended to use the ERROR level because logging has an impact on performance. More information about log4j can be found at `http://logging.apache.org/log4j`.

To help understand how logging works and also how the hierarchy of logging levels will behave with the tests that we will make, I have made a small application that has all the log levels and it will be printed according to the settings made when the application is called.

It is available in the same repository as the applications used in the previous topic. We will access the directory and make a build and deploy the application. This application is called app2-v01-logging, as shown in the following code:

```
[root@wfly_book wfly_book]# cd /opt/book_apps/wfly_book/app2-v01-logging/
[root@wfly_book app2-v01-logging]# mvn wildfly:deploy
```

At this time, we will not make any changes in the WildFly logging configuration, but will only access the application at `http://<your-server-address:8080/log/home`, as shown in the following screenshot.

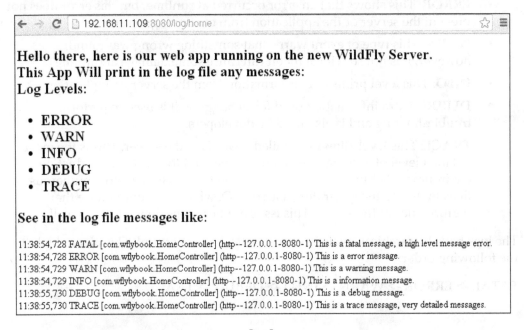

Note that in the `WildFly` logs printed messages, the `DEBUG` and `TRACE` levels were not printed:

`FATAL [com.wflybook.HomeController] (default task-5) This is a fatal message, a high level message error.`

`ERROR [com.wflybook.HomeController] (default task-5) This is a error message.`

`WARN  [com.wflybook.HomeController] (default task-5) This is a warning message.`

`INFO  [com.wflybook.HomeController] (default task-5) This is a information message.`

This happened because of the hierarchy, as, with the INFO level enabled, all the levels above it will be printed. In order to print DEBUG or TRACE you need to configure them. Let's configure the the TRACE level so that all logs are printed. To do so, change the `standalone.xml` file as follows and then restart the WildFly server:

```
<root-logger>
    <level name="TRACE"/>
    <handlers>
        <handler name="CONSOLE"/>
        <handler name="FILE"/>
    </handlers>
</root-logger>
```

Note that several TRACE messages were printed. This is because we changed the root logger to TRACE, which means we will use the TRACE level for all the events that are generated. As we want to enable TRACE level only for our application, we must create a logger for our application. For this, change the root logger to INFO again and perform the following configuration in the `standalone.xml` file:

```
<logger category="com.wflybook.HomeController">
    <level name="TRACE"/>
</logger>

<root-logger>
    <level name="INFO"/>
    <handlers>
        <handler name="CONSOLE"/>
        <handler name="FILE"/>
    </handlers>
</root-logger>
```

The category field should be filled with the class you want to use. In this case, all the classes that belong to the `com.wflybook.HomeController` context will register the TRACE level log events. Now, it will print all the levels when we call the application again as shown in the following output:

```
FATAL [com.wflybook.HomeController] (default task-1) This is a fatal
message, a high level message error.

ERROR [com.wflybook.HomeController] (default task-1) This is a error
message.

WARN  [com.wflybook.HomeController] (default task-1) This is a warning
message.

INFO  [com.wflybook.HomeController] (default task-1) This is a
information message.

DEBUG [com.wflybook.HomeController] (default task-1) This is a debug
message.

TRACE [com.wflybook.HomeController] (default task-1) This is a trace
message, very detailed messages.
```

It is necessary that all logs of a particular application are generated in a separate file, or that all error logs are printed in another file. In short, all these configurations are possible, but it's necessary to create a handler to define how these messages will be saved. For example, we will use the same application and configure a handler only for it; therefore, all the messages from our application will also be written in a separate file. We will create a handler for this test using the following code:

```
<file-handler name="APP2-TEST">
  <level name="TRACE"/>
  <formatter>
    <named-formatter name="COLOR-PATTERN"/>
  </formatter>
  <file relative-to="jboss.server.log.dir" path="app2-v01.log"/>
  <append value="true"/>
</file-handler>
```

Now, change the logger that we created earlier so that it looks similar to the following code:

```
<logger category="com.wflybook.HomeController">
  <handlers>
    <handler name="APP2-TEST"/>
  </handlers>
</logger>
```

Save the file and restart theWildFly server:

```
[root@wfly_book app2-v01-logging]# service wildfly restart
Stopping wildfly:                                    [  OK  ]
Starting wildfly:                                    [  OK  ]
```

Note that the configured handler generated the log file as expected:

```
[root@wfly_book app2-v01-logging]# ls /opt/server/wildfly-8.0.0.CR1/
standalone/log/

app2-v01.log  server.log
```

Now, access the application again and see that the logs referring only to our application were written:

```
[root@wfly_book ~]# cat  /opt/server/wildfly-8.0.0.CR1/standalone/log/
app2-v01.log
```

```
FATAL [com.wflybook.HomeController] (default task-1) This is a fatal
message, a high level message error.
ERROR [com.wflybook.HomeController] (default task-1) This is a error
message.
WARN  [com.wflybook.HomeController] (default task-1) This is a warning
message.
INFO  [com.wflybook.HomeController] (default task-1) This is a
information message.
DEBUG [com.wflybook.HomeController] (default task-1) This is a debug
message.
TRACE [com.wflybook.HomeController] (default task-1) This is a trace
message, very detailed messages.
```

Installing MySQL modules

In order to install new modules in WildFly, we need to create a directory for the new module following the pattern of the directories inside $ JBOSS_HOME/modules. You must have a library (JAR) and module.xml file that describes the module itself and its dependencies from other modules, if any.

To illustrate how to create a new module, we will create a module to be used by datasources that we will use in subsequent chapters. Let's start. First, get the MySQL JAR file, available at http://dev.MySQL.com/downloads/connector/j/.

Creating the directory to create the module

To create a new module, we must follow the WildFly patterns. This mechanism creates a single default location under which modules can be located easily. For this, access the base directory under `/opt/server/wildfly-8.0.0.CR1/modules/system/layers/`.

So, within the subdirectory `com`, let's create the necessary structure for the MySQL module installation as follows:

`[root@wfly_book main]# mkdir -p com/mysql/jdbc/main`

The directory does not need to be exactly like this; however, for easy identification of a module, we follow the package hierarchy. For example, a module that has the following hierarchy `com.spolti.modules.MyModule.class` would look like this `com/spolti/modules/main`.

This is not a rule, but rather a standard that is adopted within the hierarchy of the WildFly modules. The directory structure of a new module can be named the way you want, but it is not a good practice. So, let's proceed with the configuration.

Copy the MySQL JAR into the directory we created previously as follows:

`[root@wfly_book main]# cd com/mysql/jdbc/main`

`[root@wfly_book main]# cp /root/MySQL-connector-java-5.1.21-bin.jar .`

Now, you must create the `module.xml` file containing information about the module as follows:

`[root@wfly_book main]# vim module.xml`

The `module.xml` file contains the following code:

```
<?xml version="1.0" encoding="UTF-8"?>
<module xmlns="urn:jboss:module:1.0" name="com.mysql.jdbc">
  <resources>
      <resource-root path="MySQL-connector-java-5.1.21-
    bin.jar"/>
  </resources>
  <dependencies>
      <module name="javax.api"/>
      <module name="javax.transaction.api"/>
  </dependencies>
</module>
```

The dependencies of the modules are basically a dependency of a class when we use the `import javax.api` command. If the module requires some dependence and the same is not declared, the module will be loaded; however, when it is used a `ClassNotFound` error may occur.

The command that must contain the directory after the settings are made is as follows:

```
[root@wfly_book main]# ls

module.xml   MySQL-connector-java-5.1.21-bin.jar
```

Now, we can start WildFly. During the startup logs we can verify whether the module has started successfully:

```
INFO  [org.jboss.as.connector.subsystems.datasources] (ServerService
Thread Pool -- 28) JBAS010404: Deploying non-JDBC-compliant driver
class com.MySQL.jdbc.Driver (version 5.1)
```

From this moment on, we have the MySQL driver available for use.

Datasources

As with all application servers, you must have a data source to manage JDBC connections to a database. The JDBC API is a standard that defines how the databases are accessed by Java applications. An application references a previously configured datasource in the application server, which in turn is associated with a JDBC driver so that the application can perform transactions in the database. The correct version of the JDBC connector directly gives the correct functioning of the datasource. As with previous versions such as JBoss, Wildfly includes a small database, the H2. It is a lightweight relational database and is also an example of a datasource for the platform. As in JBoss AS 7, the datasources are all defined within the subsystem `datasources`. This subsystem is subdivided into two parts, listed as follows:

- **Datasources**: This is where the datasources are configured
- **Drivers**: This is the session where the list of drivers used by the datasources is configured

For the installation of a driver, we have the following two possible methods:

- **Module**: In this mode, the driver must be installed as a module into WildFly as we did already.

- **Deploy**: In this mode, simply deploy the driver as if it were an application. If this driver is in the default JDBC4 pattern, WildFly will recognize the driver immediately. See the following example present in the `domain.xml` or `standalone.xml` configuration file:

```
<datasources>
  <datasource jndi-name="java:jboss/datasources/ExampleDS" pool-
    name="ExampleDS" enabled="true" use-java-context="true">
  <connection-url>jdbc:h2:mem:test;DB_CLOSE_DELAY=-1;DB_CLOSE_ON_
EXIT=FALSE</connection-url>
  <driver>h2</driver>
  <security>
        <user-name>sa</user-name>
        <password>sa</password>
  </security>
</datasource>
<drivers>
  <driver name="h2" module="com.h2database.h2">
    <xa-datasource-class>org.h2.jdbcx.JdbcDataSource</xa-
      datasource-class>
  </driver>
</drivers>
```

Let's configure a datasource. Assuming that we already have a MySQL database driver installed, we will configure a datasource, and edit the file, in our case, the `standalone.xml` file:

```
[root@wfly_book standalone]# vim /opt/server/wildfly-8.0.0.CR1/
standalone/configuration/standalone.xml
```

In the datasources subsystem, configure the datasource and the driver that will be used by this datasource, as shown in the following code:

```
<datasource jta="true" jndi-name="java:/ExampleMysqlDS" pool-
  name="ExampleMysqlDS" enabled="true" use-java-context="true">
  <connection-url>jdbc:mysql://localhost:3306/ExampleMysql </
connection-
    url>
  <driver>mysqlExample</driver>
  <pool>
    <min-pool-size>10</min-pool-size>
    <max-pool-size>10</max-pool-size>
  </pool>
  <security>
        <user-name>example</user-name>
        <password>example</password>
```

```
    </security>
  </datasource>
```

Let's understand each of the fields mentioned in the previous code:

- `jndi-name`: This field specifies the JNDI name for the datasource subsystem
- `pool-name`: This field specifies the pool name for the datasource subsystem used for management
- `enabled`: This field says whether the datasource subsystem is active or not
- `use-java-context`: Setting this field to false will bind the dataSource subsystem into global JNDI
- `connection-url`: This is the JDBC driver connection URL
- `driver`: This is the driver name used by this datasource
- `min-pool-size`: This is the number of the connections that this pool will establish with the database
- `max-pool-size`: This element indicates the maximum number of connections for a pool
- `user-name`: This is the database username
- `password`: This is the password used by the `datasource` subsystem to connect into database

In the `Name` field, it must be configured with the same name that is given to the driver. Enter the configuration of the MySQL driver, as shown in the following code:

```
<driver name="mysqlExample" module="com.mysql.jdbc">
  <xa-datasource-class>com.mysql.jdbc.jdbc2.optional.
    MysqlXADataSource</xa-datasource-class>
</driver>
```

To verify if the `datasource` subsystem was deployed, execute the following command. The name of the created `datasource` must be shown in the output to know that it is deployed.

Keep in mind that the WildFly server must be running.

```
[root@wfly_book ~]# /opt/server/wildfly-8.0.0.CR1/bin/jboss-cli.sh -c
--command="ls /subsystem=datasources/data-source="

ExampleDS

ExampleMysqlDS
```

Note that our new datasource is now created and deployed.

Crypt datasource passwords

It is always a good practice to protect passwords, especially when it comes to production, as contained within them is certainly very crucial information for your business, and we do not want this data to be exposed in any way. The encryption used in the JBoss project is asymmetric, which means that, after encryption, it cannot be decrypted again without a password or key. This is one more layer on the application server, if accessed by people who are not allowed to do so, with the intention of obtaining restricted information. In this case, the encryption of datasource passwords will help. Even if an attacker gets access to your application server instance, he will be unable to access the db instance, which is typically located on a different, physical host. Let's see what the necessary steps to encrypt the database password are.

For everything to work, you must create a security-domain inside the security subsystem. We will now explain how this works:

It can also be done using the WildFly Security Vault, a facility of PicketBox that allows you to mask sensitive attributes such as passwords. Much more details can be found at `https://github.com/wildfly/quickstart/tree/master/security-vault-askpass`.

```
[root@wfly_book standalone]# vim /opt/server/wildfly-8.0.0.CR1/
standalone/configuration/standalone.xml
```

```xml
<security-domain name="ExampleMysqlDSRealm">
  <authentication>
    <login-module code="SecureIdentity" flag="required">
      <module-option name="username" value="your-database-
        username"/>
      <module-option name="password" value="encrypted-password"/>
      <module-option name="managedConnectionFactoryName"
        value="jboss.jca:name= ExampleMysqlDS,service=XATxCM"/>
    </login-module>
  </authentication>
</security-domain>
```

And after the configured security domain, it is necessary to include in between the `<security>` and the `</security>` tags on field for the login and password of the datasource subsystem as shown in the following code:

```xml
<security-domain>Your-Security-Domain-Name</security-domain>
```

After implementing the above settings, the data source will look similar to the following code:

```
<datasource jta="true" jndi-name="java:/ExampleMysqlDS" pool-name="
ExampleMysqlDS " enabled="true" use-java-context="true">
  <connection-url>jdbc:mysql://localhost:3306/ExampleMysql </
connection-
    url>
  <driver> mysqlExample </driver>
  <pool>
    <min-pool-size>10</min-pool-size>
    <max-pool-size>10</max-pool-size>
  </pool>
  <security>
    <security-domain>ExampleMysqlDSRealm</security-domain>
  </security>
</datasource>
```

Now we can encrypt any password and enter it at the previously performed configuration. I have made a small application to help do this task. To use it, go to the directory we created earlier for the applications and then enter the corresponding directory to the JAR file. Then perform the build shown as follows:

```
[root@wfly_book wfly_book]# cd /opt/book_apps/wfly_book/app2-ds-wildfly/

[root@wfly_book app2-ds-wildfly]# mvn package
```

Use the JAR file created in the target directory to encrypt and decrypt the passwords as follows:

```
[root@wfly_book app2-ds-wildfly]# java -jar target/app2-ds-wildfly.jar
encode testPassword

By Spolti

6562a2557e676509c3bc376bef610c0a
```

To configure the encrypted password in the datasource, copy the generated hash and make the modification to the security domain file, `ExampleMysqlDSRealm`, as follows:

```
<module-option name="password"
  value="6562a2557e676509c3bc376bef610c0a"/>
```

Other configurations

A properly configured server is the basis of any operation today. By default, WildFly already protects the management interfaces as they are only available for local access. The settings listed in the following sections are one of them, something like the first steps in the server configuration. It is clear that WildFly is a server that has many complex settings but that is not the focus of this book.

Accessing the management console for the first time

WildFly as well as JBoss AS 7 has a security level that restricts access to the management console by IP source. By default, it only accepts connections locally through the loopback address or localhost (127.0.0.1). If you are using the same machine that is running WildFly, it is not necessary to change the bind IP to access the management console. However, if you are using another machine, you must perform a configuration to be able to access the management console remotely.

There are two ways to perform this configuration as follows:

- Startup parameters: These are available only for the current execution. If the WildFly server is restarted, this configuration must be set again.

- Editing `standalone|domain.xml`: This is a permanent configuration.

First, we perform the configuration parameters via the WildFly startup as follows:

```
[root@wfly_book bin]# ./standalone.sh -Djboss.bind.address.
management=192.168.11.109
```

Note that in the logs the IP address has changed as shown in the following commands:

```
INFO  [org.jboss.as] (Controller Boot Thread) JBAS015961: Http management
interface listening on http://192.168.11.109:9990/management
INFO  [org.jboss.as] (Controller Boot Thread) JBAS015951: Admin console
listening on http://192.168.11.109:9990
```

And permanently in the `standalone.xml` or `domain.xml` configuration file, change this section as follows:

```
<interface name="management">
  <inet-address value=
    "${jboss.bind.address.management:127.0.0.1}"/>
</interface>
<interface name="management">
  <inet-address value="${jboss.bind.address.management:
    192.168.11.109}"/>
</interface>
```

Regardless of how you chose to configure it to access the management console, use the URL `http://<your-ip-addrress>:9990` to perform access

Notice that we were instantly redirected to an error page instructing us to create a user to be able to use the console, as shown in the following screenshot:

Continue on this page to obtain a step-by-step walk-through on how to perform this procedure:

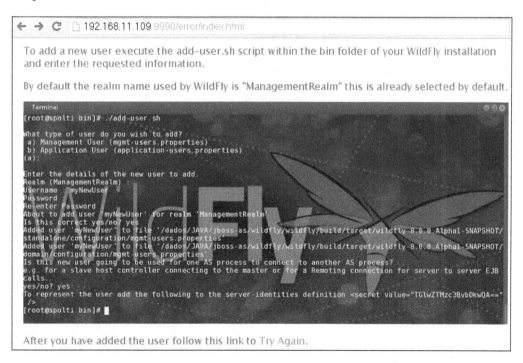

The script, as described in *Chapter 1, Starting with Wildfly,* is in the bin directory. Access it and run it as follows:

```
[root@wfly_book ~]# cd /opt/server/wildfly-8.0.0.CR1/bin/
[root@wfly_book bin]# ./add-user.sh
```

The command-line output obtained is as follows:

```
What type of user do you wish to add?
 a) Management User (mgmt-users.properties)
 b) Application User (application-users.properties)
(a):
```

At this point, answer a and press *Enter* to select option **a) Management User**.

```
. . .
About to add user 'example' for realm 'ManagementRealm'
Is this correct yes/no? yes
```

Answer yes for the previous question and press *Enter*.

```
Added user 'example' to file '/opt/server/wildfly-8.0.0.CR1/standalone/
configuration/mgmt-users.properties'
Added user 'example' to file '/opt/server/wildfly-8.0.0.CR1/domain/
configuration/mgmt-users.properties'
Added user 'example' with groups PowerUser,BillingAdmin to file '/opt/
server/wildfly-8.0.0.CR1/standalone/configuration/mgmt-groups.properties'
Added user 'example' with groups PowerUser,BillingAdmin to file '/opt/
server/wildfly-8.0.0.CR1/domain/configuration/mgmt-groups.properties'
Is this new user going to be used for one AS process to connect to
another AS process?
e.g. for a slave host controller connecting to the master or for a
Remoting connection for server to server EJB calls.
yes/no? yes
```

Answer yes to the previous question.

```
To represent the user add the following to the server-identities
definition <secret value="bGlwZTMzc3BvbDkwQA==" />
```

Upon completion of the creation of a new user, click on the link at the end of the page:

> After you have added the user follow this link to Try Again

You will be prompted for authentication. Enter the username and password you created in the previous procedure, and you will see the main part of the management console as shown in the following screenshot:

Configuring e-mail

In virtually all applications that are developed for different purposes, there is always the need to send e-mails, whether for information, to reset user passwords, among others. This configuration is not complicated to perform in the WildFly Server. The configuration through the `standalone.xml` file is performed in two steps. First, you must create a mail session inside the `mail` subsystem; second, create an outbound socket binding within the socket binding group at the end of the `standalone.xml` file. First, we create the mail session, to access this `standalone.xml` configuration file and include the following configuration within the mail subsystem:

```
<mail-session name="ExampleGmail" jndi-name="java:jboss/mail/
ExampleGmail">
  <smtp-server ssl="true" outbound-socket-binding-ref="mail-gmail-
    smtp" username="exemple@gmail.com" password="secret"/>
</mail-session>
```

This is as follows:

```
<subsystem xmlns="urn:jboss:domain:mail:2.0">
  <mail-session name="default" jndi-name="java:jboss/mail/Default">
    <smtp-server outbound-socket-binding-ref="mail-smtp"/>
  </mail-session>
  <mail-session name="ExampleGmail" jndi-
    name="java:jboss/mail/ExampleGmail">
    <smtp-server ssl="true" outbound-socket-binding-ref="mail-gmail-
      smtp" username="exemple@gmail.com" password="secret"/>
  </mail-session>
</subsystem>
```

Now, create the outbound socket binding for the mail session you have created. This setting should be inserted at the end of the file between the tags and `<socket-binding-group> </ socket-binding-group>`, as follows:

```
<socket-binding-group name="standard-sockets" default-
  interface="public" port-offset="${jboss.socket.binding.port-
    offset:0}">
  <socket-binding name="management-native" interface="management"
    port="${jboss.management.native.port:9999}"/>
  <socket-binding name="management-http" interface="management"
    port="${jboss.management.http.port:9990}"/>
  <socket-binding name="management-https" interface="management"
    port="${jboss.management.https.port:9993}"/>
  <socket-binding name="ajp" port="${jboss.ajp.port:8009}"/>
  <socket-binding name="http" port="${jboss.http.port:8080}"/>
  <socket-binding name="https" port="${jboss.https.port:8443}"/>
  <socket-binding name="txn-recovery-environment" port="4712"/>
  <socket-binding name="txn-status-manager" port="4713"/>
  <outbound-socket-binding name="mail-smtp">
      <remote-destination host="localhost" port="25"/>
  </outbound-socket-binding>
  <outbound-socket-binding name="mail-gmail-smtp">
      <remote-destination host="smtp.gmail.com" port="465"/>
  </outbound-socket-binding>
</socket-binding-group>
```

Restart WildFly so that the settings are applied. Then, access the management console and check whether the e-mail configuration has been successfully applied and whether it is shown in the Mail tab as shown in the following screenshot:

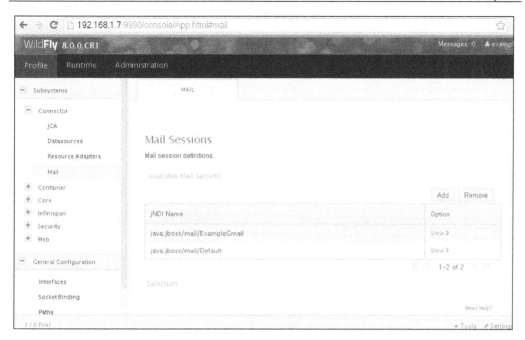

You can also perform this configuration through the management console, as we will see in subsequent chapters.

Now that you know the structure of centralized configuration in WildFly more deeply, we can focus on adjusting the settings via the CLI and management console. Yes, you can also make all the settings without them by directly editing the configuration files, but these tools are certainly extremely useful and greatly simplify the administration.

Summary

This chapter showed you details about the main settings and configuration procedures. You learned a lot about deployments and the deployment scanner that uses file marks and how to easily control the deployment and find out about its status.

This chapter has shown us the importance of the logging subsystems and discussed the possibility of segregating logs of applications in different files or just increasing or decreasing the level of detail of the log. It also addressed datasource configuration and how to keep your database password secure from being accessed by a third party.

3
WildFly CLI and Management Console

In WildFly, as well as in the versions of JBoss 7, all server instances and settings are managed through the **Command-line Interface** (**CLI**) and management console instead of editing the XML files. But as we have seen earlier, it is also possible to implement all settings by editing the XML files. Administration through the management interfaces provides an extra validation and advanced features for managing. The main difference between the two methods, manual editing via the Console and CLI, is that the changes made by editing the XML files will be applied only when the server is re-started, whereas some of the changes made through the console are applied even if the server is running.

Connecting to the CLI

The CLI is an administration tool usable by the command line to perform tasks in the WildFly Application server. With the CLI, we can perform diverse administrative actions, such as deploy and undeploy, the stop and change settings, and the system parameters. There is also an interesting option in the CLI that is able to perform actions in the batch mode, which means it can be multitasked like a script. The CLI is able to perform all the administrative operations, whereas the management console can only deal with a part of them.

The CLI is a command-line environment; to use it, you need to run a script that is located in the `bin` folder of the WildFly installation. The name of the script is `jboss -cli.sh`, but soon it will be renamed. Let's access it with WildFly already running. If it is not running, start WildFly and then run the script as follows:

```
[root@wfly_book wildfly-8.0.0.CR1]# servicewildfly start
[root@wfly_book wildfly-8.0.0.CR1]# cd /opt/server/wildfly-8.0.0.CR1/bin/
```

Now, execute the `jboss-cli.sh` script as follows:

```
[root@wfly_book bin]# ./jboss-cli.sh
```

The output of the preceding command is as follows:

```
You are disconnected at the moment. Type 'connect' to connect to the
server or 'help' for the list of supported commands.
[disconnected /]
```

Due to the preceding result of the executed command, type `connect` to connect to the server using the CLI as follows:

```
[disconnected /] connect
[standalone@localhost:9990 /]
```

In this way, we are connected locally. When we need to connect on a domain controller or on another host, we can follow two methods. The first method is as follows:

```
[root@wfly_book bin]# ./jboss-cli.sh
You are disconnected at the moment. Type 'connect' to connect to the
server or 'help' for the list of supported commands.
[disconnected /] connect localhost:9990
[standalone@localhost:9990 /]
```

The second method is by using the following command line:

```
[root@wfly_book bin]# ./jboss-cli.sh --connect
--controller=localhost:9990
[standalone@localhost:9990 /]
```

To become familiar with the CLI, we can use the `help` command to see a list of available commands and also to see the help for a given command, as shown in the following output:

```
[standalone@localhost:9990 /] help --commands
Commands available in the current context:
```

batch	connect	deployment-overlay	history
module	read-attribute	set	unset
cd	data-source	echo	if
patch	read-operation	shutdown	version
clear	deploy	echo-dmrjdbc-driver-info	pwd
reload	try	xa-data-source	
command	deployment-info	help	ls
quit	run-batch	undeploy	

```
To read a description of a specific command execute 'command_name
--help'.
```

In order to get help for a specific command, use the following syntax:

```
command_name -help
```

Refer to the following example:

```
[standalone@localhost:9990 /] echo --help
```

The output of the preceding command is as follows:

```
SYNOPSIS

echo ($name)*


DESCRIPTION

Prints values for the specified variables.
    If the command is executed w/o arguments then the command will print
all the existing variables with their values in the name=value format.

ARGUMENTS

Optional whitespace-separated sequence of variable names.
```

To exit the CLI, simply type quit in the command line as follows:

```
[standalone@localhost:9990 /] quit

[root@wfly_book bin]#
```

Creating a datasource with the CLI and management console

WildFly has extensive configuration options, which can be accomplished by manually editing configuration files, using the REST API, using the CLI, and using the management console. The last two options are addressed in the upcoming section. The CLI replaces the twiddle present in the earlier versions of AS 7 such as JBoss 4 and 5, which was also a utility via command line but with far fewer resources. Today, with the CLI, you can perform any administrative task. In the next topic, we will address some settings and the ways to perform them in the CLI and the management console.

Creating a datasource using the CLI

The steps to use the CLI are as follows:

1. Connect the CLI.

2. Create the datasource.

3. Activate the datasource.

   An example of the full command where we can change variables to the desired value is given as follows:

   ```
   [standalone@localhost:9990 /] data-source add --name=TesteCliDS
   --jndi-name=java:/TesteCliDS --driver-name=mysql --connection-
   url=jdbc:mysql://localhost:3306/testeCli --user-name=testecli
   --password=changeme
   ```

4. See the logs that confirm that the datasource has been created and enabled as follows:

   ```
   JBAS010400: Bound data source [java:/TesteCliDS]
   ```

5. Now, let's check the standalone.xml or domain.xml configuration file as follows to see whether the datasource has been created:

   ```
   <datasourcejndi-name="java:/TesteCliDS" pool-
     name="TesteCliDS" enabled="false">
     <connection-url>jdbc:mysql://localhost:3306/testeCli
     </connection-url>
     <driver>mysql</driver>
     <security>
       <user-name>testecli</user-name>
       <password>changeme</password>
     </security>
   </datasource>
   ```

To disable the datasource, use the following command line:

```
[standalone@localhost:9990 /] data-source --name=TesteCliDS disable
operation-requires-reload: true
process-state:              reload-required
```

To remove the datasource, just repeat the preceding command and use the remove parameter as follows:

```
[standalone@localhost:9990 /] data-source --name=TesteCliDS remove
process-state: reload-required
```

We can reload the WildFLy server easily through the CLI by running the following command:

```
[standalone@localhost:9990 /] reload
```

Now, if we look at the `standalone.xml/domain.xml` file, the datasource is no longer present.

Creating a datasource using the management console

Recalling once again, for configuration of the datasource, the module of the database must already be created, as described in the previous chapter.

Let's start accessing the management console by visiting `http://<your_management_bind_address>:9990/`.

Perform the following steps:

1. Enter the previously-created credentials.
2. Click on the **Profile** tab and then immediately click on **Datasources**, as shown in the following screenshot:

3. The datasources and its options will appear. Click on the **Add** button and then fill in the fields on the screen that will open. You will be prompted for the datasource and JNDI name, as shown in the following screenshot:

4. Click on **Next** and select the driver that will be used to create the datasource, as show in in the following screenshot:

5. Now, complete the fields. The **Security Domain** field can be used if you wish to use an encrypted password for the datasource; let's fill in the fields and complete the configuration, as shown in the following screenshot:

6. You can see that the datasource was created successfully but is not yet active in the following screenshot:

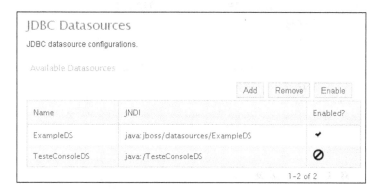

7. To activate the datasource, just select it and click on the **Enable** button, and you will be directed to a confirmation page as shown in the following screenshot:

8. Simply click on **Confirm** to apply the configuration. After confirming, check out the following log and see whether the datasource has been successfully installed:

```
JBAS010400: Bound data source [java:/TesteConsoleDS]
```

9. Check if the domain.xml file configuration or standalone.xml file has the datasource configured using the following code:

```
<datasourcejta="false" jndi-name="java:/TesteConsoleDS"
  pool-name="TesteConsoleDS" enabled="true"
    use-ccm="false">
  <connection-url>jdbc:mysql://127.0.0.1:3306/TestConsoleDS
    </connection-url>
  <driver-class>com.mysql.jdbc.Driver</driver-class>
  <driver>mysql</driver>
  <security>
    <user-name>test</user-name>
    <password>test</password>
  </security>
  <validation>
    <validate-on-match>false</validate-on-match>
    <background-validation>false</background-validation>
  </validation>
  <statement>
    <share-prepared-statements>false
      </share-prepared-statements>
```

```
        </statement>
    </datasource>
```

10. To remove the datasource, you only need to select the datasource, click on **Remove,** and then on **Confirm,** as shown in the following screenshot:

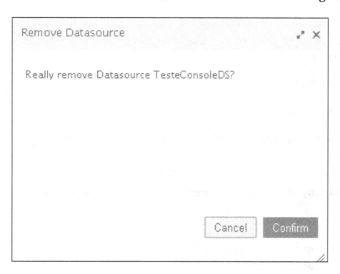

A good tip for performing the deletion by the management console is that it is not necessary to re-start the server. Just look in the logs and the files will already be removed. Refer to the following command:

```
JBAS010409: Unbound data source [java:/TesteConsoleDS]
```

Deployment with the CLI and management console

WildFly has several configuration options and ways to deploy applications. For both administrators and developers, the CLI and management console offer several options that make the job easier. For this chapter, the standalone mode will be used to perform the deployments.

Deployment with the CLI

Installation of applications using the CLI provides advantages of owning a single command-line interface that allows us to run installation scripts for specific scenarios. You can manage the status of the deployment of a single server or all servers that make up the domain. Before proceeding with the deploy, we will delete all the applications that we have deployed earlier.

Let's perform the deploy. Access the CLI using the following command:

```
[root@wfly_book bin]# ./jboss-cli.sh --connect
--controller=192.168.11.109:9990
[standalone@192.168.11.109:9990 /]
```

To deploy, just use the `deploy` command, passing the application location in the filesystem as a parameter. For the following example, we use the application `app1-v01`:

```
[standalone@192.168.11.109:9990 /] deploy app1-v01.war
```

The output of the preceding command is as follows:

```
JBAS015876: Starting deployment of "app1-v01.war" (runtime-name:
"app1-v01.war")
JBAS017534: Register web context: /app1-v01
JBAS018559: Deployed "app1-v01.war" (runtime-name : "app1-v01.war")
```

The application is now available at `http://<ip-address>:8080/app1-v01/`.

To undeploy the application using the CLI, just use the undeploy command followed by the name of the artifact. The CLI has the autocomplete attribute. If you do not remember the full name of the artifact, just press *Tab* to use the autocomplete attribute.

```
[standalone@192.168.11.109:9990 /] undeploy app1-v01.war
```

In the logs, we can see that the `undeploy` command was successfully completed as follows:

```
JBAS017535: Unregister web context: /app1-v01
JBAS015877: Stopped deployment app1-v01.war (runtime-name: app1-v01.war)
in 3566ms
JBAS014901: Content removed from location /opt/server/wildfly-8.0.0.CR1/
standalone/data/content/24/ec8acdc2610bc6b4a59d3736274d7659a21177/content
JBAS018558: Undeployed "app1-v01.war" (runtime-name: "app1-v01.war")
```

Deployment with the management console

Performing the deployment through the management console provides some advantages; the main one is ease of use. Quickly identify the applications that are installed and you can disable certain applications or even delete them at any time. The management console has a small disadvantage compared to the CLI; it does not cover all the possible configurations that can be accomplished. Perform the following steps:

1. To begin, access the management console.

2. Click on the **Runtime** tab and click on **Manage Deployments**, as shown in the following screenshot:

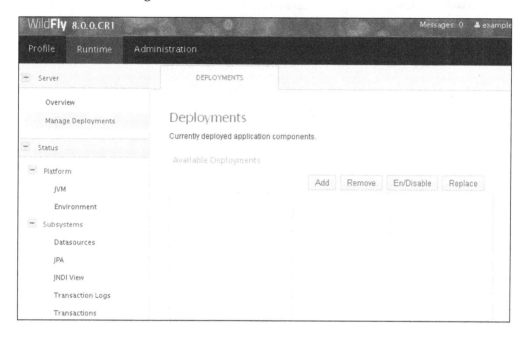

3. The preceding page displays all active deployments. In this case, we do not have any deployment; we'll add the first deployment. For this, click on the **Add** button and select the artifact to perform the deploy. In my case, I copied the artifact application, app1-v01, for my test machine desktop as shown in the following screenshot:

4. When you click on **Next**, the upload of the artifact will be performed. On the next page, change only the **Name** and **Runtime Name** values if desired. The **Name** parameter is the name that the application will have, and it will be used for access through a web browser. The **Runtime Name** parameter is the name that the application will run within the environment.

5. Click on **Save** and you can see that the application is on the server but is still inactive, as shown in the following screenshot:

6. To activate the deploy and make the application available, select the application and click on the **En/Disable** button to activate it and then click on **Confirm** to confirm the action, as shown in the following screenshot:

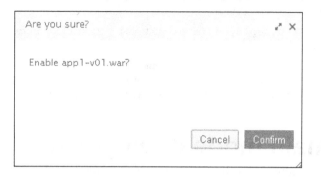

7. After the request is completed, you can check the logs that show the completion of the deployment. At this time, the application is now available for access; check the logs as follows:

   ```
   JBAS015876: Starting deployment of "app1-v01.war" (runtime-name:
   "app1-v01.war")
   ```

   ```
   JBAS017534: Register web context: /app1-v01
   ```

   ```
   JBAS018559: Deployed "app1-v01.war" (runtime-name :
   "app1-v01.war")
   ```

8. To disable the application, just click on the same button that you used to activate the deployment. Now, let's remove the application from our server. Select the application you want to remove, and click on the **Remove** button, and then on the **Confirm** button to confirm the request as shown in the following screenshot:

9. On completion of the request, we can see in the logs that the undeploy command was successful as follows:

    JBAS015877: Stopped deployment app1-v01.war (runtime-name: app1-v01.war) in 119ms

    JBAS018558: Undeployed "app1-v01.war" (runtime-name: "app1-v01.war")

    JBAS014901: Content removed from location /opt/ server/wildfly-8.0.0.CR1/standalone/data/content/24/ ec8acdc2610bc6b4a59d3736274d7659a21177/content

The domain mode deployment

First of all, I would like to emphasize that deployments based on filesystems are not supported in the domain mode. To accomplish this, we must use the CLI or the management console.

The domain mode deployment using the CLI

For the domain mode deployment using the CLI, you need to connect the CLI using the same steps performed previously to connect in the CLI.

For this example, we will use the application app1 v02.

Once logged in to the CLI, run the following command to perform the deployment:

[domain@localhost:9990 /] deploy /opt/book_apps/wfly_book/app1-v02/ target/app1-v02-0.0.1-SNAPSHOT.war --all-server-groups

Wait until the execution completes so that we can easily verify the completion of the deployment via the management console, as shown in the following screenshot:

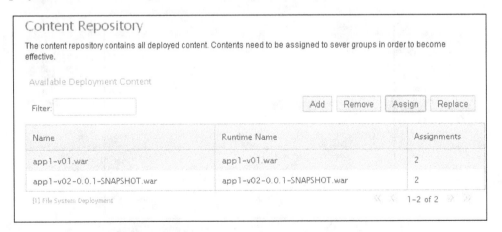

The output is as follows:

```
[Server:server-two] 18:04:18,088 INFO   [org.wildfly.extension.undertow]
(MSC service thread 1-1) JBAS017534: Register web context: /

[Server:server-two] 18:04:19,780 INFO   [org.jboss.as.server]
(Controller Boot Thread) JBAS018559: Deployed "app1-v02-0.0.1-SNAPSHOT.
war" (runtime-name : "app1-v02-0.0.1-SNAPSHOT.war")

[Server:server-two] 18:04:24,837 INFO   [org.jboss.as] (Controller Boot
Thread) JBAS015874: WildFly 8.0.0.CR1 "WildFly" started in 78666ms -
Started 301 of 353 services (94 services are lazy, passive or on-demand)

[Server:server-one] 18:04:35,469 INFO   [org.wildfly.extension.undertow]
(MSC service thread 1-2) JBAS017534: Register web context: /

[Server:server-one] 18:04:36,506 INFO   [org.jboss.as.server] (Controller
Boot Thread) JBAS018559: Deployed "app1-v02-0.0.1-SNAPSHOT.war" (runtime-
name : "app1-v02-0.0.1-SNAPSHOT.war")
```

To undeploy using the CLI, just execute the following command:

```
[domain@localhost:9990 /] undeploy app1-v02-0.0.1-SNAPSHOT.war--all-
relevant-server-groups
```

The domain mode deployment using the management console

For the domain mode deployment using the management console, you need to start WildFly in the domain mode. For this, run the following command:

```
[root@wfly_book ~]# /opt/server/wildfly-8.0.0.CR1/bin/domain.sh
```

Once WildFly is running, open the management console, the procedure and the user are the same used in the previous example for the standalone mode.

Let's begin, accessing the management console by visiting http://<your_ management_bind_address>:9990/ using your browser and type your username and password, which you have created previously.

To start the deployment, perform the following steps:

1. Click on **Manage Deployments**, and then on **Add** as shown in the following screenshot:

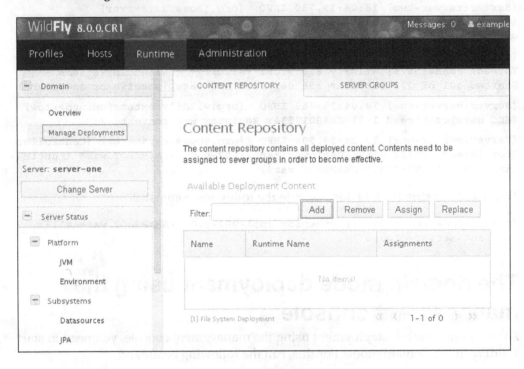

2. Now, select the file to perform the deploy, and then click on **Next**, as shown in the following screenshot:

3. Then, just click on **Save** as shown in the following screenshot:

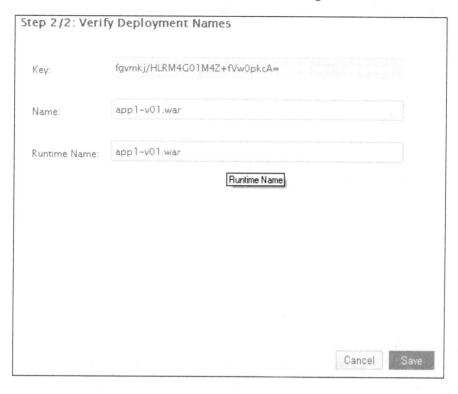

4. After the artifact is added, it is necessary to assign the deployment to a server group. For this, click on the server groups, and then on **Assign**:

5. Now, you need to select the artifact. We will select the artifact that we added earlier, and then click on **Save**, as shown in the following screenshot:

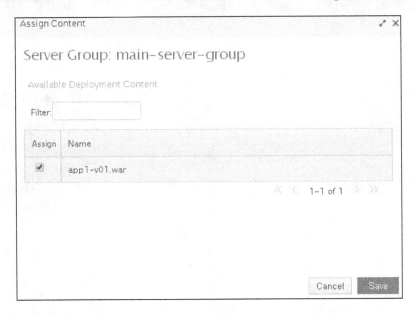

6. And lastly, you must enable the deployment. For this, select the artifact and click on **En/Disable** as shown in the following screenshot:

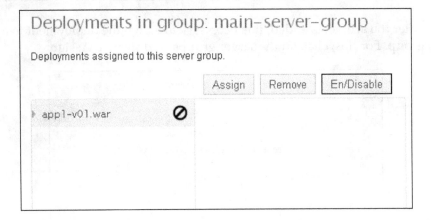

7. Confirm the action and wait till the end of the deployment.

8. The deployment will be carried out for all instances that are part of the group server. Check the following logs and notice that the deployment was performed:

```
[Server:server-two] 16:52:49,559 INFO  [org.jboss.as.server]
(host-controller-connection-threads - 4) JBAS018559: Deployed
"app1-v01.war" (runtime-name : "app1-v01.war")
```

```
[Server:server-one] 16:52:49,335 INFO  [org.jboss.as.server]
(host-controller-connection-threads - 4) JBAS018559: Deployed
"app1-v01.war" (runtime-name : "app1-v01.war")
```

9. And to undeploy, just click on **En/Disable** again.

Configuring e-mail via the CLI and management console

Sending e-mails from any application is an important point because it is through this that many applications send notifications to users or administrators. It is often used to reset passwords and to register new users in almost all the sites or applications. We can thus understand that e-mail is a key service that we have to set up in our application server. Throughout this rest of chapter, we will see how to configure e-mails through the CLI and the management console.

E-mail setup via the CLI

To begin the setup, we need to define the e-mail server that we will use, whether it is internal or external, the sender of e-mails, and the JNDI name. For this example, I will configure a mail session with the following parameters:

- **Mail session**: `java:/mail/TestEmailCLI`
- **JNDI mail session**: `java:/mail/TestEmailCLI`
- **Field form**: `noreply@testgmail.com`

Other fields such as e-mail, username, and password, if needed, will change according to your settings. For the creation of a mail session, you must have an outbound-socket-binding set that will be the gateway used to send messages. If you do not have an outbound-socket-binding set, configure it as follows, connecting to the CLI:

```
[root@wfly_book bin]# ./jboss-cli.sh --connect
```

If you are already connected, run the following command in the CLI to add the outbound-socket-binding set:

```
[standalone@192.168.11.109:9990 /] /socket-binding-
group=standard-sockets/remote-destination-outbound-socket-
binding=gmailTest:add(host=smtp.gmail.com,port=993)

{"outcome" => "success"}
```

Check whether the configuration has been added into `standalone.xml` as follows:

```
<outbound-socket-binding name="gmailTest">
  <remote-destination host="smtp.gmail.com" port="993"/>
</outbound-socket-binding>
```

Now, we can add the mail session on defining the following parameters. For this, I'll split this task into two steps. First, add the mail session and then the SMTP server, as follows:

- Mail session:

  You can set up the mail session using the following command line:

  ```
  [standalone@192.168.11.109:9990 /] /subsystem=mail/mail-
  session="java:/mail/TestEmailCLI":add(jndi-name="java:/mail/
  TestEmailCLI", from="noreply@testegmail.com")

  {"outcome" => "success"}
  ```

- SMTP server:

  The SMTP server is set up using the following code:

  ```
  [standalone@192.168.11.109:9990 /] /subsystem=mail/mail-
    session="java:/mail/TestEmailCLI"/server=smtp:add
      (outbound-socket-binding-ref=gmailTest,
        password=somepass,ssl=true,username=user@gmail.com)
  {
    "outcome" => "success",
    "response-headers" => {
      "operation-requires-reload" => true,
      "process-state" => "reload-required"
    }
  }
  ```

Note that the following code has also been added in `standalone.xml`:

```
<mail-session name="java:/mail/TestEmailCLI" jndi-
  name="java:/mail/TestEmailCLI" from="noreply@testegmail.com">
```

```
<smtp-server outbound-socket-binding-ref="gmailTest" ssl="true"
    username="user@gmail.com" password="somepass"/>
</mail-session>
```

The process requests a restart, but if we check the logs, the mail-session bound has already been done. Refer to the following output:

```
JBAS015400: Bound mail session [java:/mail/TestEmailCLI]
```

Now, let's set up another mail session, but now, through the management console.

E-mail setup via the management console

With the running WildFly, access the management console, navigate to the **Profile** tab, and then click on **Mail,** as shown in the following screenshot:

Note that the mail sessions we created earlier are present. We will add one more mail session with the following parameters:

- **Mail session**: java:/mail/TestEmailConsole
- **JNDI Mail session**: java:/mail/TestEmailConsole
- **Field from**: noreply@testegmail.com

In the following screenshot of the **Create Mail Session** window, type the JNDI name in the **JNDI Name** field and click on **Save**:

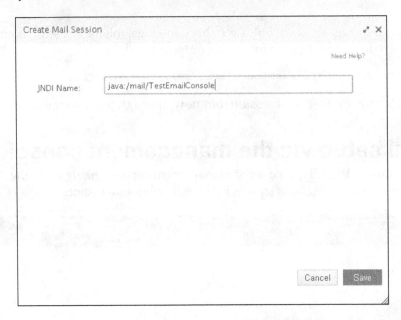

Now, we need to configure the JNDI. For this, select the JNDI created. Click on **View**, and then on the **Add** button to add the remaining settings. Then, click on **Save** as shown in the following screenshot:

See that your `standalone.xml` configuration has been applied as follows:

```
<mail-session name="java:/mail/TestEmailConsole" jndi-
  name="java:/mail/TestEmailConsole">
  <smtp-server outbound-socket-binding-ref="gmailTest" ssl="true"
    username="example@gmail.com" password="example"/>
</mail-session>
```

Refer to the following output log:

```
JBAS015400: Bound mail session [java:/mail/TestEmailConsole]
```

With the settings made regardless of the method used for performing the setup, we have a mail session configured and ready to use in our application server.

It is important that every administrator should know to perform the basic settings for the server to work as expected. This chapter prepares the reader , who sometimes lack specific knowledge, for day-to-day activities. Certainly, the book prepares the reader to receive this new technology and enables the reader to be able to prepare it to run in a production environment. My main aim is to provide the reader with a unique and very detailed experience through practical and detailed book examples.

Summary

This chapter introduces the new WildFly CLI and management console. In this chapter, we have addressed various configurations and the use of both the consoles, the CLI and management console, and how important they are for a day-to-day administration of WildFly. The management console and the CLI allow the user to connect the domain controller or a standalone server that gives us the option to perform all administrative tasks, but only with the CLI is it possible to execute all of them; the management console does not perform all the tasks.

Summary

4
Modular Services and Class Loading

WildFly, as well as JBoss AS 7, has a class loading system considerably different from the previous versions. The WildFly class loading is based on JBoss Modules. Instead of using the hierarchy of class loading that is most commonly known, WildFly class loading is based on modules that have to explicitly define their dependencies on other modules. The WildFly deployments are also in modules and do not have access to classes that are defined in JAR files on the application server unless a dependency is defined for these classes.

Class loading precedence

Even for those WildFly modules that are isolated by default as part of the deployment process, some dependencies of modules are defined by the application server transparently to the end user. In this way, it becomes transparent, which helps us to make a deployment without errors. Assuming that you are performing a Java EE application deployment, the dependencies of Java API's will be added to your application automatically. Automatic dependencies can be excluded through the use of `jboss-deployment-structure.xml`.

A very common problem of class loading in Java applications is applications that include libraries that are also provided by the container. This can result in the creation of multiple versions of the same classes in the environment and can cause problems during deployment. To prevent this type of problem, the dependencies are included in a specific order that prevents this type of error. The following is a list of dependencies arranged in the order of the highest to the lowest priority:

- **System dependencies**: These are the dependencies that are automatically added by the container, including Java APIs

- **User dependencies**: These are the dependencies that are added through `jboss-deployment-structure.xml` or through the dependencies manifest entry
- **Local resource**: These are classes packaged within the project, present in `WEB-INF/classes` or `WEB-INF/lib`
- Inter deployment dependencies: These are dependencies of other deployments of an EAR. This can include classes of the `lib` directory of an EAR or classes defined in other JARs.

WAR and EAR class loading

This topic will help us understand a little more about the class loading of applications using packaging, in the case of WAR and EAR files.

WAR class loading

Every WAR file is considered to be a single module, so all the libs that are in `WEB-INF/lib` and `WEB-INF/classes` will be treated the same way. Thus, all classes packaged along with the application will be loaded in the same class loader. For a WAR application, when using Maven, it is very practical to resolve all dependencies; for example, if your application uses the Servlet API, just add the following code on to your project POM:

```
<dependencies>
  ...
    <dependency>
      <groupId>javax.servlet</groupId>
      <artifactId>servlet-api</artifactId>
      <version>2.5</version>
    </dependency>
  ...
</dependencies>
```

However, if you wish to use the Servlet API provided by the container or by the `EAR/lib` JARs, you must configure the scope of the dependency that is provided as follows:

```
<dependencies>
  ...
    <dependency>
      <groupId>javax.servlet</groupId>
      <artifactId>servlet-api</artifactId>
      <version>2.5</version>
```

```
        <scope>provided</scope>
    </dependency>
    ...
</dependencies>
```

Let's look inside one of our applications used throughout this book and check all the libraries with normal dependency and then with the provided scope. For that, we will use the first app, app1-v01. First just run the application build as follows:

```
[root@wfly_book ~]# cd /opt/book_apps/wfly_book/app1-v01/
[root@wfly_book app1-v01]# mvn clean package
```

Next, check the libs that were added to the project:

```
[root@wfly_book app1-v01]# ls target/app1-v01/WEB-INF/lib/
javaee-api-6.0.jar  servlet-api-2.5.jar
```

We have two libraries. Now, let's set the the lib servlet-api as provided and see what happens.

Edit the pom.xml file for this project to become the lib provided and add the following configuration for the dependency lib that we will change:

```
<scope>provided</scope>
```

The dependency should be as follows:

```
<dependency>
<groupId>javax.servlet</groupId>
<artifactId>servlet-api</artifactId>
<version>2.5</version>
<scope>provided</scope>
</dependency>
```

Save the file and run the build package again:

```
[root@wfly_book app1-v01]# mvn clean package
```

Wait for the end and check the libs that were added in the application again:

```
[root@wfly_book app1-v01]# ls target/app1-v01/WEB-INF/lib/
javaee-api-6.0.jar
```

Notice that there is more to the servlet-apilib. This is because the configuration made for Maven says that the lib will be provided by the web server or container and need not be present in this Classloader application. If no container is provided, there arises a ClassNotFound error.

EAR class loading

EAR deployments are multimodule deployments. This means not all the classes that are within the EAR will have access to all other classes of the EAR, unless a dependency is defined. For example, if we have one lib that will be used by all other subdeployments within the EAR app, then there is no need to declare it in each module. We can define a dependency on Class Path using the MANIFEST file in the EAR file. Let's use the example of log4j; we will set it to be exported to all other subdeployments. For this, it is necessary to use the MANIFEST file to create the dependency. It is possible to do it manually or use Maven to create it. I particularly prefer using Maven and consider this to be a best practice. To use Maven, just add the following configuration in the pom.xml file of the application already informing the dependency that we want configure:

```
<build>
...
<plugins>
  <plugin>
  <artifactId>maven-war-plugin</artifactId>
  <configuration>
    <archive>
      <manifestEntries>
        <Dependencies>org.slf4j</Dependencies>
      </manifestEntries>
    </archive>
  </configuration>
  </plugin>
</plugins>
</build>
```

By default, the lib folder inside the EAR is a single module, and each deployment of a WAR or EJB module is separated. All subdeployments have dependence on its parent module, which provides access to classes that are in the lib folder of EAR, but they do not always have automatic dependency on each of them. This behavior is controlled by the ear-deployment-isolated configuration in the: jboss : domain : ee subsystem, as shown in the following code:

```
<subsystem xmlns="urn:jboss:domain:ee:2.0">
  <ear-subdeployments-isolated>false</ear-subdeployments-isolated>
  ...
</suvsystem>
```

Or you can do that using the `jboss-deployment-structure.xml` file, using exactly the same key. Observe the following code:

```
<jboss-deployment-structure>
...
<ear-subdeployments-isolated>true</ear-subdeployments-isolated>
...
</jboss-deployment-structure>
```

This parameter is set to `false` by default. This allows other artifacts that are within EAR to see each other. You can see the `.ear` artifact in the following screenshot:

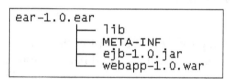

If the `ear-subdeployment-isolated` parameter is set to `False`, all the WAR and JAR classes will access each other. It is important to remember that `ear-sub deployments` or an isolated classloader configuration will not take effect in WARs that are outside the EAR file. Anyway it will have its own classloader applications. And on the other hand, if the parameter is set to `true`, no dependency on any module is automatically set, so all the dependencies have to be handled manually as specified by the user in the `Class Path` project or by specifying module dependencies. Let's see whether it works.

First, deploy the last example app, `app4-v01`. Access the app directory using the following command:

[root@wfly_book app4-v01]# cd /opt/book_apps/wfly_book/app4-v01/

Now, deploy the app using the following command:

[root@wfly_book app4-v01]# mvn package

Then, copy the EAR file to the WildFly deployment directory as follows:

[root@wfly_book app4-v01]# cp ear/target/ear-1.0.ear /opt/server/ wildfly-8.0.0.CR1/standalone/deployments/

So, in order to access the app through the web browser and watch the WildFly log, use the URL `http://<your-ip-address>:8080/test`.

Note that the log messages from the servlet were printed as expected:

```
14:27:51,558 INFO   [com.ear.MyServlet] (default task-1) Our test
Servlet was accessed

14:27:51,854 INFO   [com.ear.MyServlet] (default task-1) Fri Mar 28
14:27:51 BRT 2014
```

Now, let's remove the `jcraft` lib from the application so that it is not bundled inside the EAR, so we can simulate the `ClassNotFound` error. In order to do that, edit the `pom.xml` file of the EAR using the following command:

```
[root@wfly_book app4-v01]# gedit ear/pom.xml
```

Then, remove the following code snippet:

```
<dependency>
<groupId>com.jcraft</groupId>
<artifactId>jsch</artifactId>
<version>0.1.48</version>
</dependency>
```

Save the file and redo the deploy. Once the deploy starts, note that an exception is thrown, a `ClassNotFound` error. This happened because the `.war` could not find the `lib` folder that was previously provided by EAR. The following is the error displayed:

```
2014-03-28 15:26:31,870 ERROR [org.jboss.msc.service.fail] (MSC service
thread 1-2) MSC000001: Failed to start service jboss.deployment.
subunit."ear-1.0.ear"."webapp-1.0.war".POST_MODULE: org.jboss.msc.
service.StartException in service jboss.deployment.subunit."ear-
1.0.ear"."webapp
-1.0.war".POST_MODULE: JBAS018733: Failed to process phase POST_MODULE
of subdeployment "webapp-1.0.war" of deployment "ear-1.0.ear"

at org.jboss.as.server.deployment.DeploymentUnitPhaseService.start(Deploy
mentUnitPhaseService.java:166) [wildfly-server-8.0.0.CR1.jar:8.0.0.CR1]

at org.jboss.msc.service.ServiceControllerImpl$StartTask.startService(Ser
viceControllerImpl.java:1948) [jboss-msc-1.2.0.CR1.jar:1.2.0.CR1]

at org.jboss.msc.service.ServiceControllerImpl$StartTask.
run(ServiceControllerImpl.java:1881) [jboss-msc-1.2.0.CR1.jar:1.2.0.CR1]

at java.util.concurrent.ThreadPoolExecutor.runWorker(ThreadPoolExecutor.
java:1145) [rt.jar:1.7.0_45]

at java.util.concurrent.ThreadPoolExecutor$Worker.run(ThreadPoolExecutor.
java:615) [rt.jar:1.7.0_45]

atjava.lang.Thread.run(Thread.java:744) [rt.jar:1.7.0_45]

Caused by: java.lang.RuntimeException: JBAS018757: Error
getting reflective information for class com.ear.MyServlet with
ClassLoaderModuleClassLoader for Module "deployment.ear-1.0.ear.webapp-
1.0.war:main" from Service Module Loader

at org.jboss.as.server.deployment.reflect.DeploymentReflectionIndex.getC
lassIndex(DeploymentReflectionIndex.java:72) [wildfly-server-8.0.0.CR1.
jar:8.0.0.CR1]

at org.jboss.as.ee.metadata.MethodAnnotationAggregator.runtimeAnnotationI
nformation(MethodAnnotationAggregator.java:58)
```

```
at org.jboss.as.ee.component.deployers.InterceptorAnnotationProcessor.han
dleAnnotations(InterceptorAnnotationProcessor.java:107)

at org.jboss.as.ee.component.deployers.InterceptorAnnotationProcessor.pro
cessComponentConfig(InterceptorAnnotationProcessor.java:92)

at org.jboss.as.ee.component.deployers.InterceptorAnnotationProcessor.dep
loy(InterceptorAnnotationProcessor.java:77)

at org.jboss.as.server.deployment.DeploymentUnitPhaseService.start(Deploy
mentUnitPhaseService.java:159) [wildfly-server-8.0.0.CR1.jar:8.0.0.CR1]

        ... 5 more
Caused by: java.lang.NoClassDefFoundError: com/jcraft/jsch/JSchException

at java.lang.Class.getDeclaredFields0(Native Method) [rt.jar:1.7.0_45]

atjava.lang.Class.privateGetDeclaredFields(Class.java:2397) [rt.
jar:1.7.0_45]

atjava.lang.Class.getDeclaredFields(Class.java:1806) [rt.jar:1.7.0_45]

at org.jboss.as.server.deployment.reflect.ClassReflectionIndex.<init>(Cla
ssReflectionIndex.java:57) [wildfly-server-8.0.0.CR1.jar:8.0.0.CR1]

at org.jboss.as.server.deployment.reflect.DeploymentReflectionIndex.getC
lassIndex(DeploymentReflectionIndex.java:68) [wildfly-server-8.0.0.CR1.
jar:8.0.0.CR1]

        ... 10 more
Caused by: java.lang.ClassNotFoundException: com.jcraft.jsch.
JSchException from [Module "deployment.ear-1.0.ear.webapp-1.0.war:main"
from Service Module Loader]

at org.jboss.modules.ModuleClassLoader.findClass(ModuleClassLoader.
java:197) [jboss-modules.jar:1.3.0.Final]

at org.jboss.modules.ConcurrentClassLoader.performLoadClassUnchecked(Conc
urrentClassLoader.java:443) [jboss-modules.jar:1.3.0.Final]

at org.jboss.modules.ConcurrentClassLoader.performLoadClassChecked(Concur
rentClassLoader.java:431) [jboss-modules.jar:1.3.0.Final]

at org.jboss.modules.ConcurrentClassLoader.performLoadClass(ConcurrentCla
ssLoader.java:373) [jboss-modules.jar:1.3.0.Final]

at org.jboss.modules.ConcurrentClassLoader.
loadClass(ConcurrentClassLoader.java:118) [jboss-modules.jar:1.3.0.Final]
        ... 15 more
```

Additionally, to configure your server to perform the SSH connection using this app and change the file MyServlet.java located under webapp/src/main/java/com/ear:

```
session = jsch.getSession("Your-Linux-User", "Your-Linux-Host",
  22);
session.setPassword("Your-Linux-Password");
```

Defining a dependency through WAR

Applications sometimes become very large due to the amount of libs that the application references. A very cool way to decrease the number of libs a project uses is to use the resources of the application server. In previous versions, it was possible to insert the libs in the `lib` folder and in the common directory of JBoss. In JBoss 7 and WildFly, we can create our own modules with one or more libs and then configure an explicit dependence through the `jboss.deployment-structure` file. First, let's prepare our application.

Then, we perform the application build designated for this example.

Access the directory of the application, `app2-v02-module`, present in the same directory used in the previous chapters, using the following command:

`[root@wfly_bookwfly_book]# cd /opt/book_apps/wfly_book/app2-v02-module/`

Deploy the application using the following command:

`[root@wfly_book app2-v02-module]# mvnwildfly:deploy`

Now, access the application and see what happens using the following URL:

`http://<your-ip-address>:8080/ssh`

As you can see in the following screenshot, the server returns an internal error:

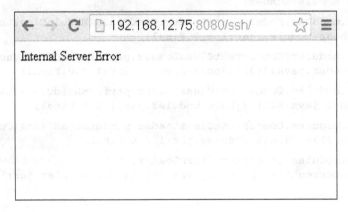

And, we can see a `ClassNotFound` error in the logs. This was because the dependency is as provided in `pom.xml`; the classloader of this module (application) is not found in the container `jsch` lib:

```
2014-03-28 16:40:00,824 ERROR [io.undertow.request] (default task
-1) UT005023: Exception handling request to /ssh/: java.lang.
NoClassDefFoundError: com/jcraft/jsch/JSchException
```

First, let's add the module in the `jsch` lib in the WildFly. To do this, go to the default directory for modules in WildFly:

```
[root@wfly_book ~]# cd /opt/server/wildfly-8.0.0.CR1/modules/system/
layers/base/
```

Now, you need to create the directory where we will store the new module. Remember that the directory that I'll create will not have a rule to be followed. But, to make it easier to understand, the `jcraft` lib is following the structure `com.jsch`. We will now create the directory, `com/jsch`, and then we will create the module with the same name. To begin the configuration, navigate to the default modules directory in WildFly and then access the `com` subdirectory using the following command:

```
[root@wfly_book base]# cd com/[root@wfly_book base]# cd com/
```

Then, create the following directory:

```
[root@wfly_book com]# mkdir -p jsch/main
```

The JAR file that will be used is available in the directory that contains the applications used; copy it to the newly created directory using the following command:

```
[root@wfly_book com]# cp /opt/book_apps/wfly_book/jsch-0.1.48.jar
jsch/main/
```

Access the directory using the following command:

```
[root@wfly_book com]# cd -p jsch/main
```

Now you need to create the module descriptor. For this, create the `module.xml` file with the following code:

```xml
<?xml version="1.0" encoding="UTF-8"?>
<module xmlns="urn:jboss:module:1.1" name="com.jsch">
  <resources>
    <resource-root path="jsch-0.1.48.jar"/>
  </resources>
  <dependencies>
    <module name="javax.api"/>
  </dependencies>
</module>
```

An important point that we must know is that there is a need to define the dependency on the artifact for the module to be loaded for this project. This will occur when we configure the jboss-deployment-structure.xml file that is present in the project's WEB-INF directory; it must contain the name of the module as shown in the following code:

```
<?xml version="1.0" encoding="UTF-8"?>
<jboss-deployment-structure>
  <deployment>
      <dependencies>
        <module name="com.jsch" />
      </dependencies>
  </deployment>
</jboss-deployment-structure>
```

You must enter javax.api as the dependency.

Create the jboss-deployment-structure.xml file:

```
[root@wfly_book app2-v02-module]# geditsrc/main/webapp/WEB-INF/jboss
-deployment-structure.xml
```

Undeploy the latest app using the following command:

```
[root@wfly_book com]# mvnwildfly:undeploy
```

Now, restart the WildFly server and then rebuild and deploy the app using the following commands:

```
[root@wfly_book com]# servicewildfly restart
[root@wfly_book com]# mvnwildfly:deploy
```

Then, test the app again; check the logs and see the logs generated by the app as shown in the following commands:

```
14:27:51,558 INFO  [com.ear.MyServlet] (default task-1) Our test Servlet
was accessed

14:27:51,854 INFO  [com.ear.MyServlet] (default task-1) Fri Mar 28
14:27:51 BRT 2014
```

If the module name is wrong in the jboss.deployment-structure.xml file, an error similar to the following will appear in the logs:

```
ERROR [org.jboss.msc.service.fail] (MSC service thread 1-5) MSC000001:
Failed to start service jboss.module.service."deployment.app2-v01-
logging-2.0.1-SNAPSHOT.war".main: org.jboss.msc.service.StartException
in service jboss.module.service."deployment.app2-v01-logging-2.0.1-
SNAPSHOT.war".main: JBAS018759: Failed to load module: deployment.app2
-v01-logging-2.0.1-SNAPSHOT.war:main
```

```
    at org.jboss.as.server.moduleservice.ModuleLoadService.
start(ModuleLoadService.java:91) [wildfly-server-8.0.0.CR1.jar:8.0.0.CR1]

    at org.jboss.msc.service.ServiceControllerImpl$StartTask.startService(S
erviceControllerImpl.java:1948) [jboss-msc-1.2.0.CR1.jar:1.2.0.CR1]

    at org.jboss.msc.service.ServiceControllerImpl$StartTask.
run(ServiceControllerImpl.java:1881) [jboss-msc-1.2.0.CR1.jar:1.2.0.CR1]

    at java.util.concurrent.ThreadPoolExecutor.
runWorker(ThreadPoolExecutor.java:1145) [rt.jar:1.7.0_17]

    at java.util.concurrent.ThreadPoolExecutor$Worker.
run(ThreadPoolExecutor.java:615) [rt.jar:1.7.0_17]

    atjava.lang.Thread.run(Thread.java:722) [rt.jar:1.7.0_17]

Caused by: org.jboss.modules.ModuleNotFoundException: 1com.jsch:main

    atorg.jboss.modules.Module.addPaths(Module.java:1030) [jboss-modules.
jar:1.3.0.Final]

    atorg.jboss.modules.Module.link(Module.java:1386) [jboss-modules.
jar:1.3.0.Final]

    atorg.jboss.modules.Module.relinkIfNecessary(Module.java:1414) [jboss-
modules.jar:1.3.0.Final]

    atorg.jboss.modules.ModuleLoader.loadModule(ModuleLoader.java:242)
[jboss-modules.jar:1.3.0.Final]

    at org.jboss.as.server.moduleservice.ModuleLoadService.
start(ModuleLoadService.java:70) [wildfly-server-8.0.0.CR1.jar:8.0.0.CR1]

    ... 5 more
```

```
ERROR [org.jboss.as.controller.management-operation] (Controller
Boot Thread) JBAS014613: Operation ("deploy") failed - address:
([("deployment" => "app2-v01-logging-2.0.1-SNAPSHOT.war")]) - failure
description: {"JBAS014671: Failed services" => {"jboss.module.
service.\"deployment.app2-v01-logging-2.0.1-SNAPSHOT.war\".main"
=> "org.jboss.msc.service.StartException in service jboss.module.
service.\"deployment.app2-v01-logging-2.0.1-SNAPSHOT.war\".main:
JBAS018759: Failed to load module: deployment.app2-v01-logging-2.0.1-
SNAPSHOT.war:main

Caused by: org.jboss.modules.ModuleNotFoundException: 1com.jsch:main"}}
```

Note that the error has launched a ModuleNotFound exception, which means
the application has not found a module called 1com.wfly eBook-app2.app2-v02
-module. It is always important to implement the settings very carefully in order
to avoid common mistakes.

Global modules

WildFly can configure any module as a global module, just like AS7. This means it can be accessed by any application or other entity within the container at any time, but it is possible that the global module is in standby until it is used. Global modules are present in the `standalone.xml` or in the `domain.xml` files. The configuration responsible for these kinds of modules is within the subsystem, `: jboss: domain: ee: 2.0`. The creation of a global module is made in two stages: the creation of a module and the configuration of the global module.

In this topic, we will see what is required to add a global module and how to configure it.

To perform this configuration is very simple. After the module is configured correctly by following the standards, just enter the configuration inside the subsystem `urn: jboss: domain: ee: 2.0` as follows:

```
<subsystem xmlns="urn:jboss:domain:ee:2.0">
<global-modules>
   <module name="module.name"/>
  </global-modules>
...
</subsystem>
```

Here, the `module.name` must be entered in the name of the newly made configuration.

This task requires us to restart WildFly. In the next section, we will see how to configure a module. Let's see one example.

Using the same application from the previous topic, remove the `jboss-deployment-structure.xml` file of the project:

```
[root@wfly_book app2-v02-module]# rm -rfsrc/main/webapp/WEB-INF/jboss-deployment-structure.xml
```

Now, edit the `standalone.xml` file and, inside the `jboss:domain:ee:2.0` subsystem, add the `jsch global module` between the tags `<global-modules>` and `</global-modules>`, as follows:

```
<global-modules>
<module name="org.javassist" slot="main"/>
<module name="com.jsch"/>
</global-modules>
```

Now, undeploy the previous app and restart the WildFly server using the following commands:

```
[root@wfly_book app2-v02-module]#mvnwildfly:undeploy
```

```
[root@wfly_book app2-v02-module]#servicewildfly restart
```

Then, deploy the application, making sure that the `jboss-deployment-structure. xml` file was removed:

```
[root@wfly_book app2-v02-module]#mvnwildfly:deploy
```

Access the application through the browser and then immediately check the logs and see that the Servlet was accessed and not declared as any dependence of the lib `jsch` in our project. So, we are using the global module that we have created using the following commands:

```
2014-03-28 18:40:31,908 INFO  [com.wflybook.HomeController] (default
task-2) Our test Servlet was accessed
```

```
2014-03-28 18:40:35,291 INFO  [com.wflybook.HomeController] (default
task-2) Fri Mar 28 18:40:35 BRT 2014
```

Summary

This chapter discussed a small range of the new class loaders that were first implemented in JBoss 7 and remained in WildFly due to its wide acceptance, performance, and friendly structure. One of the positives is the reduction of errors in class loading, which was in fact a big headache when these errors occurred in the previous versions of JBoss AS. The concept of modules is connected directly to a subdeployment. For example, each JAR, WAR, or EAR file is considered as a subdeployment and each has its own class loader, unless this is explicitly configured as discussed in this chapter. We have seen that, in a module, we can include one or more libraries; it helps us to group several libraries. Our application needs only one module and a dependency defines this application. We have also seen what the global modules are and how they work.

5
Memory and Thread Pool Management

The Java Virtual Machine (JVM) is the most important part of a Java application, because it is the part that will run our application and store all your classes, objects, and methods. In this chapter, we delve a little deeper into the JVM and learn to change the parameters used by the JVM, such as memory and **Garbage Collection** (**GC**). It is important to note that there are spaces in the JVM memory. We will see how the memory area is divided and what the function of each area is. When we run our applications, we do not know, in fact, what happens internally within the JVM. Virtually, all issues, particularly the GC and memory allocation, pass unnoticed. This chapter will help us understand more about the importance that the JVM has to an application in terms of performance and other points.

Learning about the JVM memory – Oracle JDK

The highest level divisions of the JVM memory are the most well known areas, such as heap and non heap. The heap area is used to store the objects instantiated from the classes, which means when an object is created from the constructor of the class it is allocated in heap memory. Let us understand what each area of memory is and why the JVM is divided into two parts—heap and non heap.

Heap memory

The heap memory is subdivided into three areas as follows:

- **The Eden generation**: This area is also known as the new generation. It is the area of memory used to, as its name already states, create new objects, except very ones. This area is constantly swept by a type of GC, the GC minor, which eliminates the short-lived objects that are the majority of the objects created. To scale this particular area of the heap memory, it is necessary to use the `-XX:NewSize` and `-XX:MaxNewSize` parameters.

- **The survival generation**: This is the area of memory used by the GC minor to store the objects that could not be removed because they have some reference. The objects stored here have a higher cyclic life. This area is very small and works as a deposit. This area can be changed by the `-XX:SurvivorRatio` parameter.

- **The old generation**: This generation is also known as the **tenured generation**. This memory area is where the objects with a higher lifecycle survive to GC of the young generation. Conventional GC, which operates the Eden and survival area, does not collect in this area; it is the full GC that sweeps across the heap memory.

To increase the heap memory size, we should use the `-Xms` and `-Xmx` parameters. In this chapter, we will see how you can make changes to these settings in the heap memory of WildFly.

Nonheap memory

Nonheap memory is divided into two parts, namely permanent generation and code cache as follows:

- **Permanent generation**: This area is responsible for storing the references to the objects in the JVM permanent generation (classes and methods) whose de-allocation is very rare or nonexistent

- **Code cache**: The HotSpot JVM also includes a code cache, containing memory that is used for compilation and storage of the native code

The stack size parameter is very important if you are running WildFly on a server with low memory, especially in a 32-bit OS; this value can be resized by using the `-Xss` parameter on the JVM startup, for example, `-Xss512k`. To change the size of the nonheap area, it is necessary to use the `-XX:PermSize` and `-XX:MaxPermSize` parameters.

The following screenshot illustrates the memory area and the parameters used for each of them in detail:

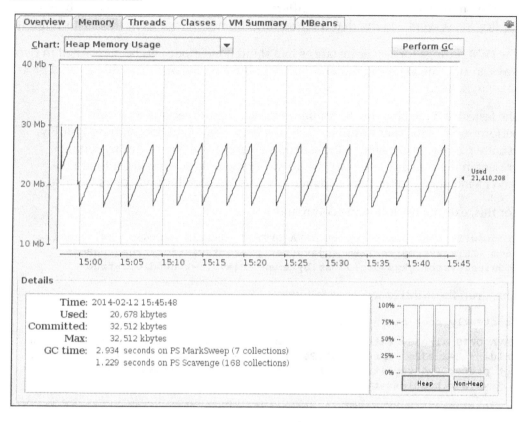

In the preceding screenshot, we can clearly see the separation of the highlighted areas of the heap and nonheap memory. The following screenshot illustrates the areas of memory in detail:

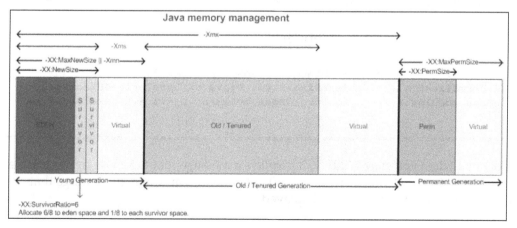

Configuring WildFly

WildFly, in this respect, is not very different from what we already know about other application servers. I know that these settings do not change from JBoss 7 to WildFly.

The JVM settings for server instances in a standalone mode can be performed in two ways: at runtime via the command line or in the `standalone.conf` file located at `$JBOSS_HOME/`.

The fastest and the best way to configure the settings, especially if we are performing specific tests or tuning tests, is via the command line, starting WildFly, usually passing parameters to the startup script that will overwrite any settings present in the `standalone.conf` file. In this first example, we will configure the server's memory and the nonheap memory. First, export the `JAVA_OPTS` variable.

For this, execute the following command:

```
[root@wfly_book bin]# export JAVA_OPTS=" -Xms32m -Xmx63m -XX:PermSize
=64m -XX:MaxPermSize=128m -Djava.net.preferIPv4Stack=true -DJBoss.
modules.system.pkgs=org.JBoss.byteman -Djava.awt.headless=true"
```

Then, run the WildFly server as follows:

```
[root@wfly_book bin]# ./standalone.sh
JAVA_OPTS already set in environment; overriding default settings with
values:  -Xms32m -Xmx63m -XX:PermSize=64m -XX:MaxPermSize=128m -Djava.
net.preferIPv4Stack=true -DJBoss.modules.system.pkgs=org.JBoss.byteman
-Djava.awt.headless=true

=========================================================================

JBoss Bootstrap Environment

  JBOSS_HOME: /opt/server/wildfly-8.0.0.CR1

JAVA: /usr/java/jdk1.7.0_45/bin/java

  JAVA_OPTS:  -server -XX:+UseCompressedOops  -Xms32m -Xmx63m
-XX:PermSize=64m -XX:MaxPermSize=128m -Djava.net.preferIPv4Stack=true
-DJBoss.modules.system.pkgs=org.JBoss.byteman -Djava.awt.headless=true

=========================================================================
```

Note that when you start WildFly, it displays a message that the `JAVA_OPTS` variable was overwritten with our new settings. Just below that message, the settings that WildFly will use for booting are displayed.

In WildFly, you can also check the state of the JVM memory using the CLI. Let's use this function in order to verify the changes made; it brings us information about all the areas of memory, such as size, and memory in use. To verify using the CLI, access it as follows:

```
[root@wfly_book bin]# ./JBoss-cli.sh --connect
--controller=192.168.11.109:9990
```

For a basic search, we can use the following command, which will list the general use of the memory heap and nonheap. Refer to the following command:

```
[standalone@192.168.11.109:9990 /] /core-service=platform-mbean/
type=memory:read-resource(include-runtime=true)
{
    "outcome" => "success",
    "result" => {
        "heap-memory-usage" => {
            "init" => 67108864L,
            "used" => 33980464L,
            "committed" => 65273856L,
            "max" => 518979584L
        },
        "non-heap-memory-usage" => {
            "init" => 24313856L,
            "used" => 43134304L,
            "committed" => 44630016L,
            "max" => 318767104L
        },
        "object-name" => "java.lang:type=Memory",
        "object-pending-finalization-count" => 0,
        "verbose" => false
    }
}
```

You can also get information about certain areas of memory, heap or nonheap, with much more detail. In this example, we will use the old or tenured generation area. The syntax of the command is as follows:

```
/core-service=platform-mbean/type=memory-pool/name=<MemoryArea>:read
-resource
```

So, to verify the tenured generation area, simply run the preceding command syntax by changing `<MemoryArea>` as `Tenured_Gen`, as follows:

```
[standalone@192.168.11.244:9990 /] /core-service=platform-mbean/
type=memory-pool/name=Tenured_Gen:read-resource
{
    "outcome" => "success",
    "result" => {
        "name" => "Tenured_Gen",
        "type" => "HEAP",
        "valid" => true,
        "memory-manager-names" => ["MarkSweepCompact"],
        "usage-threshold-supported" => true,
        "collection-usage-threshold-supported" => true,
        "usage-threshold" => 0L,
        "collection-usage-threshold" => 0L,
        "usage" => {
            "init" => 44761088L,
            "used" => 21658104L,
            "committed" => 44761088L,
            "max" => 357957632L
        },
        "peak-usage" => {
            "init" => 44761088L,
            "used" => 24110616L,
            "committed" => 44761088L,
            "max" => 357957632L
        },
        "usage-threshold-exceeded" => false,
        "usage-threshold-count" => 0L,
        "collection-usage-threshold-exceeded" => false,
        "collection-usage-threshold-count" => 0L,
        "collection-usage" => {
            "init" => 44761088L,
            "used" => 19494520L,
            "committed" => 44761088L,
            "max" => 357957632L
        },
```

```
        "object-name" => "java.lang:type=MemoryPool,name=\"Tenured
            Gen\""

    }

}
```

Another way to change the parameters of the JVM startup is through the `standalone.conf` file.

All the settings made in this file become permanent; that is, the settings will be maintained at all times even if WildFly restarts.

We declared the `JAVA_OPTS` variable in the previous example. Now, run the following command to clear the variable:

```
[root@wfly_book bin]# unset JAVA_OPTS
```

Let's change the heap and nonheap memory the same way as we did in the preceding example. For this, edit the `standalone.conf` file using the following command:

```
[root@wfly_book bin]# vimstandalone.conf
```

Edit the following command line:

```
JAVA_OPTS="-Xms64m -Xmx512m -XX:MaxPermSize=256m -Djava.net.
preferIPv4Stack=true"
```

Include the `-XX:PermSize` parameter as follows:

```
JAVA_OPTS="-Xms32m –Xmx64m -XX:PermSize=64m -XX:MaxPermSize=128m -Djava.
net.preferIPv4Stack=true"
```

Save the file and start WildFly. Note that we have the changed values also. Refer to the following command:

```
[root@wfly_book bin]# ./standalone.sh
==========================================================================

JBoss Bootstrap Environment

  JBOSS_HOME: /opt/server/wildfly-8.0.0.CR1

JAVA: /usr/java/jdk1.7.0_45/bin/java

  JAVA_OPTS:   -server -XX:+UseCompressedOops -Xms32m -Xmx64m
-XX:PermSize=64m -XX:MaxPermSize=128m -Djava.net.preferIPv4Stack=true
-DJBoss.modules.system.pkgs=org.JBoss.byteman -Djava.awt.headless=true
==========================================================================
```

In the next section, we will understand a little more about GC and the ways to improve performance through parameterization.

Garbage Collector and tuning

Garbage collector is an automatic memory manager of the JVM that works by freeing memory blocks that are no longer used by the application. Any object in the heap memory, which cannot be accessed by any active thread, is eligible for garbage collection. This means that the object will be collected so that the garbage collector runs. To help us better understand how the garbage collector works, we'll use a small application that stores the objects in the heap memory. Watching the memory can clearly monitor the implementation of the garbage collector. This application is in the directory used by the previous applications.

We will have to build the WAR to begin the test. Navigate to the directory and compile the application as follows:

```
[root@wfly_book app3-v01-memory-test]# cd /opt/book_apps/wfly_book/
app3-v01-memory-test/
[root@wfly_book app3-v01-memory-test]# mvn install
```

Perform the application deployment. After the deployment has been completed, access the application through http://your_ip:8080/app3/home.

Before accessing the application, we will open JConsole to monitor the memory consumption during the execution of the JVM.

The following are the methods to open JConsole:

- **Linux**: $JBOSS_HOME/bin/jconsole.sh
- **Windows**: "%JBOSS_HOME%/bin/jconsole.bat"

To access the application, let's use the jconsole.sh|bat script present in the $JBOSS_HOME/ bin. This is necessary because it uses several libraries and rewrites the CLASSPATH variable by entering all the necessary libraries to run JConsole. For this example, I will use a Linux machine with local access.

With WildFly running, run the following command to open JConsole:

```
[root@wfly_book ~]# $JBOSS_HOME/bin/jconsole.sh
```

The window of JConsole will be opened. Now, select the WildFly process and click on **Connect** as shown in the following screenshot:

Once logged in, click on the **Memory** tab, and then run the application through the browser. So, we will see that the consumption will increase quickly and then immediately decrease, as shown in the following screenshot:

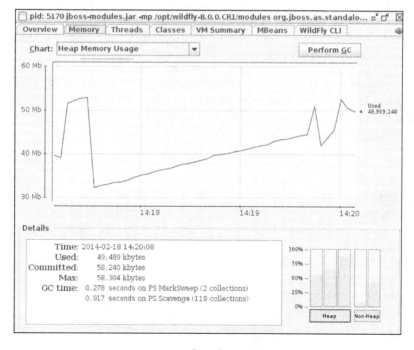

Note that the Garbage Collector runs automatically called by the JVM as shown in the following screenshot:

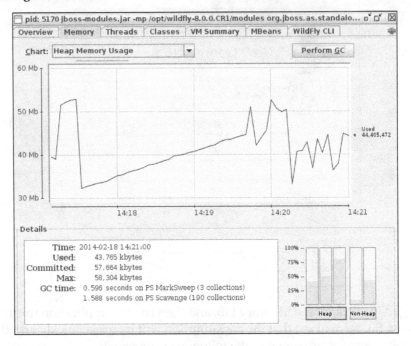

We can see that GC was performed but wasn't very effective. This is because most of the objects on the heap were still accessible or within reference of any thread. In this case, they are not able to be collected. Now, we simulate OutOfMemoryError and see what we can do to improve the JVM and GC.

Open another browser and run the application again; it will double the requests to the server thus increasing the consumption of heap, and within a few minutes, the heap memory will burst or the GC overhead limit will be exceeded. Refer to the following types of errors:

- `java.lang.OutOfMemoryError: Java Heap Space`: Basically, this error occurs when the JVM arrives at the limit of memory allocation. The basic process for resolving this error is to increase the JVM memory; however, if the memory improvement does not resolve the problem, probably you have a memory leak. Detailed information about the memory leak can be found at `http://www.oracle.com/technetwork/java/javase/memleaks-137499.html#gbywf`. A problem that occurs frequently is that the application consumes too much memory. These cases should be analyzed more carefully, identifying offenders and passing the classes with problems to the development team. To change the JVM memory, follow the steps in the *Learning about the JVM memory – Oracle JDK* section of this chapter.

- `java.lang.OutOfMemoryError: GC overhead limit exceeded`:
  The official statement of Sun for this is as follows:

  > *"The parallel collector will throw an OutOfMemoryError if too much time is being spent in garbage collection: if more than 98% of the total time is spent in garbage collection and less than 2% of the heap is recovered, an OutOfMemoryError will be thrown. This feature is designed to prevent applications from running for an extended period of time while making little or no progress because the heap is too small. If necessary, this feature can be disabled by adding the option -XX:-UseGCOverheadLimit to the command line."*

  This error is not as worrisome as the other `OutMemoryError` errors of the JVM. For more advanced users, it is interesting to perform a more detailed analysis of the GC; this can be enabled using the `-verbose:gc` parameter.

  It is also interesting to make the JVM generate a dump when an `OutOfMemory` error occurs, so it can be further analyzed. Use the `-XX:+HeapDumpOnOutOfMemoryError` parameter. To configure this option, we must just add it on the JVM startup as a parameter or you can configure into `standalone/domain.conf` too; it is your choice.

We have several other options available for JVM tuning. The following options are those that I consider the most important:

- `ParallelGC`: This option uses a few parameters. They are as follows;

  ◦ `-XX:+UseParallelGC`

  ◦ `-XX:ParallelGCThreads=value`

- `-XX:+UseCompressedOops`: This parameter is allowed only in JVM 64-bits. In the last year, most HotSpot JVMs had it by default. This option allows references to be 32-bit in a 64-bit JVM and access close to 32 GB of heap. This can save a significant amount of memory and potentially improve the performance.

- `-XX:OnOutOfMemoryError`: This parameter lets you perform an action when a memory error occurs. It is possible to restart the server. In this case, WildFly configures this parameter.

A good practice is to always leave equal memory for the parameters `Xms` and `Xmx` to avoid memory allocation errors.

The undertow HTTP pool

If you are entering the world of JBoss 7 now, this is a part of the configuration that is completely different from the previous versions. In JBoss 7, this configuration is made by referring Thread Executor; we perform the settings of the web server thread pool. Moreover, with WildFly, this setting is made; otherwise, you must use the **WORKERS** element that needs to be modified in an **IO** Subsystem. Even for me, this is a novelty. In this topic, we will learn how to perform configuration of the undertow thread pool.

Let's implement this setting using the CLI and management console. Let's start the management console by performing the following steps:

1. Start WildFly, if it has stopped, using the following command:

    ```
    [root@wfly_book bin]# servicewildfly start
    Starting wildfly:                                              [  OK
    ]
    ```

2. Now, access the management console. With the opened console, click on **Profile**, and then navigate to **Subsystems | Core | IO**, as shown in the following screenshot:

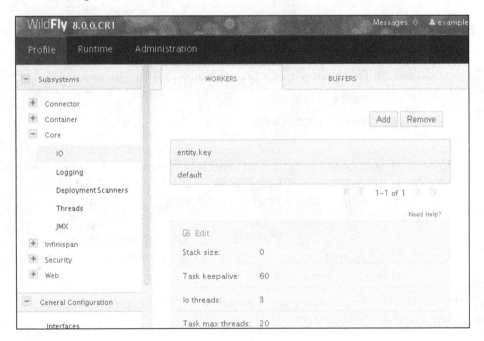

3. With the **WORKERS** tab selected, you can see that we already have an active connector, which is **default**. Let's edit it. Click on the **Edit** button, and then change the **Io threads** field (this field is responsible for the maximum number of threads allowed by undertow), as shown in the following screenshot:

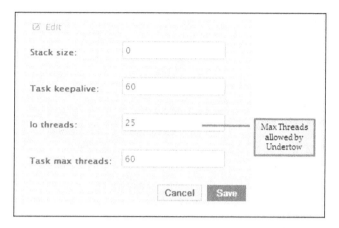

4. To make the changes, you need to restart the WildFly server.

5. Now, let's do the configuration via the command line. After WildFly restarts, access the CLI as follows:

```
[root@wfly_book bin]# ./jboss-cli.sh --connect
--controller=192.168.11.244:9990
```

6. To accomplish the configuration, simply run the following command:

```
[standalone@192.168.11.244:9990 /] /subsystem=io/
worker=default:write-attribute(name=io-threads,value=45)
(name=task-max-threads, value=45)
{
    "outcome" => "success",
    "response-headers" => {
        "operation-requires-reload" => true,
        "process-state" => "reload-required"
    }
}
```

The configuration requested us to restart the server, so we will restart.

After restarting WildFly, we check if the configuration was successfully applied.

Through the CLI, use the following command:

```
[standalone@192.168.11.244:9990 /] /subsystem=io/worker=default:
read-resource
{
    "outcome" => "success",
    "result" => {
        "io-threads" => 45,
        "stack-size" => 0L,
        "task-keepalive" => 60,
        "task-max-threads" => 45
    }
}
```

Through the management console, refer to the following screenshot:

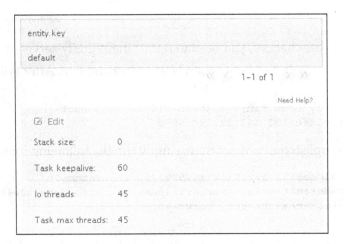

Summary

Application tuning, JVM, and application servers in the Java world are very important points and can directly impact a production or development environment. Imagine how unpleasant it is to have a JBoss or WildFly server that stops working every hour. Some basic settings are strongly recommended in these cases, such as how to properly configure the JVM memory or an HTTP connector. In this chapter, we saw various basic-level configurations that are essential to any administrators working in the Java environment. Now that you know the basics of the WildFly server, you're ready to dive insto this world and discover the true power of WildFly.

What You Need to Know – Migrating from AS 7 to WildFly 8

This is the last section of the book and will give you a brief introduction to the major changes that occurred between the servers in the JBoss AS 7 application and WildFly 8, and what you need to know to perform a migration. Yes, there are several changes between the two, but you usually need not make many changes in your application to get it to work. Keep in mind that this is not always a rule. We will deploy the applications used in this book on JBoss AS 7 and demonstrate that no errors occur.

Updated components

The new version of WildFly brought many changes, all for the better, of course, and it has many updated features, many libraries, several bugs, and problems that existed earlier and no longer exist in the WildFly final version. A big change for applications that use old libraries is that we will have to change the version of the module. A great example of this is Hibernate; many applications use Version 3 and are incompatible with the native WildFly version. Similarly, the following components have been modified in WildFly 8:

- Arquillian 1.1.2.Final-wildfly-1
- Byteman 2.1.4
- EJB Client 2.0.0.Final

- Eclipse JDT Core Compiler 4.3.1
- Groovy 2.2.1
- Hal 2.1.1.Final
- Hibernate 4.3.1.Final
- Hibernate Search 4.5.0.Final
- Hibernate Validator 5.0.3.Final
- Hornetq 2.4.1.Final
- Invocation 1.2.1.Final
- Ironjacamar 1.1.3.Final
- JBeret 1.0.0.Final
- JBoss Logging 3.1.4.GA
- JBoss Logmanager 1.5.2.Final
- JBoss Marshalling 1.4.3.Final
- JGroups 3.4.2.Final
- Jackson 1.9.13
- Jastow 1.0.0.Final
- Jipijapa 1.0.1.Final
- Log4j JBoss LogManager 1.1.0.Final
- Metadata 8.0.0.Final
- Mod_cluster 1.3.0.Final
- Mojarras 2.2.5-jbossorg-3
- Msc 1.2.0.Final
- Narayana 5.0.0.Final
- Netty 4.0.15.Final
- Netty-xnio-transport 0.1.1.Final
- PicketBox 4.0.20.Final
- PicketLink 2.5.2.Final
- Remote naming 2.0.0.Final
- Remoting 4.0.0.Final
- Remoting JMX 2.0.0.Final

- SASL 1.0.4.Final
- Santuario 1.5.6
- Undertow 1.0.0.Final
- Weld 2.1.2.Final
- Wildfly Security Manager 1.0.0.Final
- XNIO 3.2.0.Final

Major changes

One of the biggest changes incorporated in WildFly 8 was the WildFly web container. Undertow was designed to provide great performance and a huge number of simultaneous connections and, of course, not to miss the fact that WildFly is 100 percent Java EE7-certified while AS7 is Java EE6-certified.

We also have a visible improvement in the number of ports that WildFly has when compared to AS 7; so, if our application is using a specific service such as JMX Remoting, it is necessary to change this inside your application; for example, the WildFly JMX subsystem URL is `service:jmx:http-remoting -jmx://127.0.0.1:9990`.

Whereas, in JBoss AS 7, the JMX subsystem is `service:jmx:rmi:///jndi/ rmi://10.81.0.227:1090/jmxrmi`.

For example, in JBoss AS 7, we have:

```
integer portInteger = Integer.valueOf(port);
Hashtable h = new Hashtable();
JMXServiceURL address = new JMXServiceURL("service:jmx:rmi:///
jndi/rmi://"+hostname+":"+port+"/jmxrmi");
connector = JMXConnectorFactory.connect(address,null);
connection = connector.getMBeanServerConnection();
```

Whereas, in WildFly, we have:

```
integer portInteger = Integer.valueOf(port);
Hashtable h = new Hashtable();
JMXServiceURL address = new JMXServiceURL("service:jmx:http
-remoting-jmx://"+hostname+":"+port);
connector = JMXConnectorFactory.connect(address,null);
connection = connector.getMBeanServerConnection();
```

The modules directory structure

Another important point is the default modules directory; note the difference between the two:

	Module Directory
WildFly	`$JBOSS_HOME/modules/system/layers/base/`
Jboss AS 7	`$JBOSS_HOME/modules`

So, if your application uses a specific module that was present in JBoss AS 7, it should be reconfigured in WildFly on your new default modules directory.

The clustering has several changes, and you can refer to it at https://community. jboss.org/wiki/ClusteringChangesInWildfly8.

Another change can be verified on the WildFly page at http://wildfly.org/ news/2014/02/11/WildFly8-Final-Released/.

Other important things to know as well that make a difference and can generate errors are explained in the following sections.

The cargo container

If you use the cargo container, you need to check some settings that should be changed in order to make it work in WildFly. Basically, you only need to be aware of the following information:

The cargo container ID must be changed from `jboss71x` to `wildfly8x`.

For example, from the Java code, change the ID container to the following:

```
ContainerFactory.createContainer("wildfly8x"...)
```

WildFly supports Version 1.4.2 onwards, and more detailed information about cargo can be found at `http://cargo.codehaus.org/Home`.

Code changes

In some cases, it is also important to know that some source codes of the application have changed, and it is necessary to make minor adjustments to the code to ensure that the application works perfectly in WildFly; let's see some of these changes.

Singleton services

A singleton service is not in clustering anymore but instead it is a clustering server package. In addition, there is a new singleton service builder functionality that is needed to create singleton services. For more information and examples, please visit `https://community.jboss.org/wiki/ClusteringChangesInWildFly8` in the new Singleton Service Builder API section.

Using Hibernate 3

Some applications need to use Hibernate 3 and are often incompatible with the native version of WildFly. For these exceptions, we can configure the application or WildFly to use Hibernate 3.

Remember that these settings apply only to Versions 3.5 or higher, and it would be ideal to use Version 3.6.x.

Configuring your application

For this, you need to include the dependencies of Hibernate 3 in your project, and this can be done by inserting the libs in the `lib` directory of your project or through Maven. To configure this, add the following code in your `persistence.xml` file:

```
<?xml version="1.0" encoding="UTF-8"?>
<persistence xmlns="http://java.sun.com/xml/ns/persistence"
version="1.0">
  <persistence-unit name="test_pu">
      <description>Hibernate3-PU</description>
      <jta-data-source>java:jboss/datasources/testDS</jta-data-
        source>
      <properties>
        <property name="hibernate.show_sql" value="false"
          />
        <property name="jboss.as.jpa.providerModule"
          value="hibernate3-bundled" />
      </properties>
  </persistence-unit>
</persistence>
```

Configuring WildFly

For this, we need to change the Hibernate 3 module inside WildFly modules and access the Hibernate 3 module directory:

```
# cd $JBOSS_HOME/modules/system/layers/base/org/hibernate/3/
```

Copy all Hibernate 3 JARs to this directory (`hibernate3-core.jar`, `hibernate3 -commons-annotations.jar`, and `hibernate3-entitymanager.jar`).

Edit the `module.xml` file and add the `resource-root` JAR files:

 # vim module.xml

Use the information as follows:

```
<?xml version="1.0" encoding="UTF-8"?><!-- Represents the Hibernate
   3.x module   -->
<module xmlns="urn:jboss:module:1.1" name="org.hibernate" slot="3">
<resources>
   <resource-root path="jipijapa-hibernate3-1.0.1.Final.jar"/>
<resource-root path="hibernate3-core.jar"/>

<resource-root path="hibernate3-commons-
   annotations.jar"/>

<resource-root path="hibernate3-entitymanager.jar"/>

</resources>

<dependencies>
   <module name="asm.asm"/>
   <module name="javax.api"/>
   <module name="javax.annotation.api"/>
   <module name="javax.enterprise.api"/>
   <module name="javax.persistence.api"/>
   <module name="javax.transaction.api"/>
   <module name="javax.validation.api"/>
   <module name="javax.xml.bind.api"/>
   <module name="org.antlr"/>
   <module name="org.apache.commons.collections"/>
   <module name="org.dom4j"/>
   <module name="org.javassist"/>
   <module name="org.jboss.as.jpa.spi"/>
   <module name="org.jboss.jandex"/>
   <module name="org.jboss.logging"/>
   <module name="org.slf4j"/>
   <module name="org.jboss.vfs"/>
</dependencies>
</module>
```

And your `persistence.xml` file will look like the following code:

```xml
<?xml version="1.0" encoding="UTF-8"?>
<persistence xmlns="http://java.sun.com/xml/ns/persistence"
version="1.0">
  <persistence-unit name="test_pu">
    <description>Hibernate3-PU</description>
    <jta-data-source>java:jboss/datasources/testDS</jta-data-
      source>
    <properties>
      <property name="hibernate.show_sql" value="false" />
    <property name="jboss.as.jpa.providerModule"
      value="org.hibernate:3" />
    </properties>
  </persistence-unit>
</persistence>
```

Now, your application must work with Hibernate 3.

Dependencies

Another big improvement that happened in WildFly was the class loader. Now even if you have, for example, JSF in your project, there will be no conflict with the JSF lib provided by WildFly because, as we saw earlier, all deployments, by default, have your class loader isolated. However, if you are using libs that are provided by the container, an error can occur, but a version error; to solve this, just set the lib to be packaged along with the application.

Deploying the same application on two servers

Let's use the `app2-v01-logging.war` application.

The deployment occurred as expected and the logs were printed. If you remember, this app has been developed for testing with WildFly; thus, the same deployment would occur with this application if it were developed for JBoss 7, and there would be no problems. Refer to the following logs. Let's see the results when you deploy in JBoss7:

```
13:43:13,901 INFO  [br.com.caelum.vraptor.core.DefaultConverters]
(MSC service thread 1-3) Registering bundled converters
13:43:13,958 INFO  [br.com.caelum.vraptor.http.route.
```

```
DefaultRouteBuilder] (MSC service thread 1-3) /home
[ALL] -> HomeController.home(String)
```

```
13:43:13,960 INFO  [br.com.caelum.vraptor.VRaptor] (MSC service thread
1-3) VRaptor 3.3.1 successfuly initialized
```

```
13:43:13,989 INFO  [org.jboss.web] (MSC service thread 1-3) JBAS018210:
Registering web context: /log
```

```
13:43:13,997 INFO  [org.jboss.as] (MSC service thread 1-6) JBAS015951:
Admin console listening on http://127.0.0.1:9990
```

```
13:43:13,997 INFO  [org.jboss.as] (MSC service thread 1-6) JBAS015874:
JBoss AS 7.1.1.Final "Brontes" started in 4654ms - Started 184 of 264
services (78 services are passive or on-demand)
```

```
13:43:14,126 INFO  [org.jboss.as.server] (DeploymentScanner-threads - 2)
JBAS018559: Deployed "app2-v01-logging-2.0.1-SNAPSHOT.war"
```

```
13:44:14,434 INFO  [org.hibernate.validator.util.Version] (http--
127.0.0.1-8080-1) Hibernate Validator 4.2.0.Final
```

```
13:44:14,583 FATAL [com.wflybook.HomeController] (http--127.0.0.1-8080-1)
This is a fatal message, a high level message error.
```

```
13:44:14,583 ERROR [com.wflybook.HomeController] (http--127.0.0.1-8080-1)
This is a error message.
```

```
13:44:14,583 WARN  [com.wflybook.HomeController] (http--127.0.0.1-8080-1)
This is a warning message.
```

```
13:44:14,584 INFO  [com.wflybook.HomeController] (http--127.0.0.1-8080-1)
This is a information message.
```

Now, note the WildFly logs:

```
13:49:04,837 INFO  [org.wildfly.extension.undertow] (MSC service thread
1-5) JBAS017534: Register web context: /log
```

```
13:49:04,888 INFO  [org.jboss.as.server] (ServerService Thread Pool --
29) JBAS018559: Deployed "app2-v01-logging-2.0.1-SNAPSHOT.war" (runtime-
name : "app2-v01-logging-2.0.1-SNAPSHOT.war")
```

```
13:49:04,963 INFO  [org.jboss.as] (Controller Boot Thread) JBAS015961:
Http management interface listening on http://127.0.0.1:9990/management
```

```
13:49:04,963 INFO  [org.jboss.as] (Controller Boot Thread) JBAS015951:
Admin console listening on http://127.0.0.1:9990
```

```
13:49:04,963 INFO  [org.jboss.as] (Controller Boot Thread) JBAS015874:
WildFly 8.0.0.CR1 "WildFly" started in 9095ms - Started 259 of 316
services (90 services are lazy, passive or on-demand)
```

```
^[13:49:13,079 INFO  [br.com.caelum.vraptor.config.BasicConfiguration]
(default task-1) Using class br.com.caelum.vraptor.ioc.spring.
SpringProvider as Container Provider
```

```
...
```

```
13:49:13,394 INFO   [br.com.caelum.vraptor.core.DefaultConverters]
(default task-1) Registering bundled converters
```

```
13:49:13,461 INFO   [br.com.caelum.vraptor.http.route.DefaultRouteBuilder]
(default task-1) /home                                          [ALL]
-> HomeController.home(String)
```

```
13:49:13,464 INFO   [br.com.caelum.vraptor.VRaptor] (default task-1)
VRaptor 3.3.1 successfuly initialized
```

```
13:49:13,668 INFO   [org.hibernate.validator.internal.util.Version]
(default task-1) HV000001: Hibernate Validator 5.0.2.Final
```

```
13:49:13,887 FATAL [com.wflybook.HomeController] (default task-1) This is
a fatal message, a high level message error.
```

```
13:49:13,888 ERROR [com.wflybook.HomeController] (default task-1) This is
a error message.
```

```
13:49:13,888 WARN   [com.wflybook.HomeController] (default task-1) This is
a warning message.
```

```
13:49:13,888 INFO   [com.wflybook.HomeController] (default task-1) This is
a information message.
```

The only difference is that the WildFly does not load dependencies of the application until it is called; this improves the startup time of the server.

Another point that needs some attention while performing migration is the configuration files of the application, such as:

- `hibernate.properties`: This is responsible for configuring the database connection file, where the data is the URL, username, and password
- `log4j.properties`: This provides the logging configuration

In WildFly, these files must be deleted and all settings that were in it should be implemented in the `standalone/domain.xml` file. Some unexpected actions can occur, such as logs not being generated or the database connection not being configured properly if the configuration is not set and these files are not deleted. Let's take a look at an example:

I will use an example in which these files are bundled within the application mentioned previously. Recollect that, at the time of deployment, there was a warning about the datasource. This happens because of the `hibernate.properties` file:

```
09:37:34,263 INFO   [org.wildfly.extension.undertow] (MSC service thread
1-3) JBAS017534: Register web context: /hs
```

```
09:37:34,338 INFO   [org.jboss.as.server] (ServerService Thread Pool --
29) JBAS018559: Deployed "hrstatus-3.2.3.war" (runtime-name : "hrstatus
-3.2.3.war")
```

```
09:37:34,502 INFO  [org.jboss.as] (Controller Boot Thread) JBAS015961:
Http management interface listening on http://127.0.0.1:9990/management

09:37:34,503 INFO  [org.jboss.as] (Controller Boot Thread) JBAS015951:
Admin console listening on http://127.0.0.1:9990

09:37:34,503 INFO  [org.jboss.as] (Controller Boot Thread) JBAS015874:
WildFly 8.0.0.CR1 "WildFly" started in 12438ms - Started 689 of 746
services (90 services are lazy, passive or on-demand)

09:39:08,694 WARN  [org.jboss.jca.core.connectionmanager.pool.strategy.
OnePool] (default task-2) IJ000612: Destroying connection that could not
be successfully matched: org.jboss.jca.core.connectionmanager.listener.
TxConnectionListener@35ae5f80[state=NORMAL managed connection=org.
jboss.jca.adapters.jdbc.local.LocalManagedConnection@158e651d
connection handles=0 lastUse=1396442253367 trackByTx=false pool=org.
jboss.jca.core.connectionmanager.pool.strategy.OnePool@42f03929
mcp=SemaphoreArrayListManagedConnectionPool@2938d514[pool=hrStatusDS]
xaResource=LocalXAResourceImpl@37905df9[connectionListener=35ae5f80
connectionManager=70833b52 warned=false currentXid=null productName=MySQL
productVersion=5.5.36-MariaDB jndiName=java:/hrStatusDS] txSync=null]
```

After the removal of the `hibernate.properties` file from the application,
the previous message is no longer present in the logs:

```
09:37:34,263 INFO  [org.wildfly.extension.undertow] (MSC service thread
1-3) JBAS017534: Register web context: /hs

09:37:34,338 INFO  [org.jboss.as.server] (ServerService Thread Pool --
29) JBAS018559: Deployed "hrstatus-3.2.3.war" (runtime-name : "hrstatus-
3.2.3.war")

09:37:34,502 INFO  [org.jboss.as] (Controller Boot Thread) JBAS015961:
Http management interface listening on http://127.0.0.1:9990/management

09:37:34,503 INFO  [org.jboss.as] (Controller Boot Thread) JBAS015951:
Admin console listening on http://127.0.0.1:9990

09:37:34,503 INFO  [org.jboss.as] (Controller Boot Thread) JBAS015874:
WildFly 8.0.0.CR1 "WildFly" started in 12438ms - Started 689 of 746
services (90 services are lazy, passive or on-demand)

09:39:08,694 WARN  [org.jboss.jca.core.connectionmanager.pool.strategy.
OnePool] (default task-2) IJ000612: Destroying connection that could not
be successfully matched: org.jboss.jca.core.connectionmanager.listener.
TxConnectionListener@35ae5f80[state=NORMAL managed connection=org.
jboss.jca.adapters.jdbc.local.LocalManagedConnection@158e651d
connection handles=0 lastUse=1396442253367 trackByTx=false pool=org.
jboss.jca.core.connectionmanager.pool.strategy.OnePool@42f03929
mcp=SemaphoreArrayListManagedConnectionPool@2938d514[pool=hrStatusDS]
xaResource=LocalXAResourceImpl@37905df9[connectionListener=35ae5f80
connectionManager=70833b52 warned=false currentXid=null productName=MySQL
productVersion=5.5.36-MariaDB jndiName=java:/hrStatusDS] txSync=null]
```

However, we still have a problem. No application log is being generated yet. This is because there's a `log4f.properties` file within the application. We will remove this and see what happens. Check the logs now:

```
09:50:32,872 INFO  [br.com.caelum.vraptor.ioc.spring.
DefaultSpringLocator] (default task-1) Using a web application context:
Root WebApplicationContext: startup date [Wed Apr 02 09:50:18 BRT 2014];
root of context hierarchy

09:50:32,876 INFO  [br.com.caelum.vraptor.scan.WebAppBootstrapFactory]
(default task-1) No static WebAppBootstrap found.

09:50:32,877 INFO  [br.com.caelum.vraptor.config.BasicConfiguration]
(default task-1) br.com.caelum.vraptor.scanning = null

09:50:33,005 INFO  [org.springframework.web.context.support.
XmlWebApplicationContext] (default task-1) Refreshing Root
WebApplicationContext: startup date [Wed Apr 02 09:50:33 BRT 2014]; root
of context hierarchy

...

...

09:50:34,823 INFO  [br.com.caelum.vraptor.http.route.DefaultRouteBuilder]
(default task-1)

09:50:35,450 INFO  [br.com.hrstatus.controller.LoginController]
(default task-1) [ Not Logged ] URI Called: /login
```

As you can see now, all the logs of the application are printed as expected. The information on this topic is very brief and only provides the basics to guide the user during a migration. It does not talk objectively about everything because each application has its own peculiarities, and this information applies to virtually all migrations.

Index

H

handlers
  about 39
  console 39
  file 39
heap memory
  about 96
  Eden generation 96
  old generation 96
  survival generation 96
  tenured generation 96
Hibernate 3 113
hierarchical classloading 6
Host Controller process 16
host-master.xml file 13
host-slave.xml file 13
host.xml file 13

I

INFO logging level 39
installation, driver
  methods 45
installation guide 9
installation, Java 7, 8
installation, MySQL module 43
isdeploying marker 28
isundeploying marker 28

J

JAR (Java Archive) file 6, 27
Java
  installing 7, 8
Java Virtual Machine. *See* **JVM**
JBeret 5
JBoss
  about 5
  URL, for details on vote 5
JBoss AS 7 81
JConsole
  opening 102
JNDI mail session
  URL 75
Jocron 5
JVM 95

JVM memory
  about 95
  heap memory 96
  nonheap memory 96
JVM tuning
  -XX:OnOutOfMemoryError option 105
  -XX:+UseCompressedOops option 105
  ParallelGC option 105

L

Lib/ext directory 10
Log directory 11
loggers 39
logging levels
  about 39
  DEBUG 39
  ERROR 39
  FATAL 39
  INFO 39
  TRACE 39
  WARN 39
logging.properties file 12, 13
logging service 38
  working 40-43
logging subsystem
  components 39

M

Mail session
  URL 75
management console, WildFly
  accessing 50-52
  used, for configuring e-mail 77-79
  used, for creating datasource 61-65
  used, for deployment 66-69
  used, for domain mode deployment 71-75
Maven
  URL, for downloading 29
  URL, for information 30
mgmt-groups.properties file 12, 13
mgmt-users.properties file 12, 13
module creation
  directory, creating for 44, 45
modules subdirectory 10
modules directory structure, WildFly 8 112

Thank you for buying
WildFly: New Features

About Packt Publishing

Packt, pronounced 'packed', published its first book "*Mastering phpMyAdmin for Effective MySQL Management*" in April 2004 and subsequently continued to specialize in publishing highly focused books on specific technologies and solutions.

Our books and publications share the experiences of your fellow IT professionals in adapting and customizing today's systems, applications, and frameworks. Our solution based books give you the knowledge and power to customize the software and technologies you're using to get the job done. Packt books are more specific and less general than the IT books you have seen in the past. Our unique business model allows us to bring you more focused information, giving you more of what you need to know, and less of what you don't.

Packt is a modern, yet unique publishing company, which focuses on producing quality, cutting-edge books for communities of developers, administrators, and newbies alike. For more information, please visit our website: www.packtpub.com.

About Packt Open Source

In 2010, Packt launched two new brands, Packt Open Source and Packt Enterprise, in order to continue its focus on specialization. This book is part of the Packt Open Source brand, home to books published on software built around Open Source licenses, and offering information to anybody from advanced developers to budding web designers. The Open Source brand also runs Packt's Open Source Royalty Scheme, by which Packt gives a royalty to each Open Source project about whose software a book is sold.

Writing for Packt

We welcome all inquiries from people who are interested in authoring. Book proposals should be sent to author@packtpub.com. If your book idea is still at an early stage and you would like to discuss it first before writing a formal book proposal, contact us; one of our commissioning editors will get in touch with you.

We're not just looking for published authors; if you have strong technical skills but no writing experience, our experienced editors can help you develop a writing career, or simply get some additional reward for your expertise.

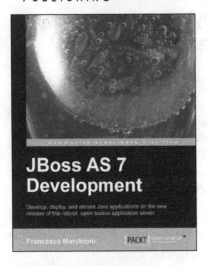

JBoss AS 7
Configuration, Deployment and
Administration

ISBN: 978-1-84951-678-5   Paperback: 380 pages

Build a fully-functional, efficient application server
using JBoss AS

1. Covers all JBoss AS 7 administration topics in
   a concise, practical, and understandable
   manner, along with detailed explanations
   and lots of screenshots.

2. Uncover the advanced features of JBoss AS,
   including High Availability and clustering,
   integration with other frameworks, and
   creating complex AS domain configurations.

JBoss EAP6 High Availability

ISBN: 978-1-78328-243-2   Paperback: 166 pages

Leverage the power of JBoss EAP6 to successfully
build high-availability clusters quickly and efficiently

1. A thorough introduction to the new
   domain mode provided by JBoss EAP6.

2. Use mod_jk and mod_cluster with
   JBoss EAP6.

3. Learn how to apply SSL in a
   clustering environment.

Please check **www.PacktPub.com** for information on our titles